Writing across the curriculum

Year 4

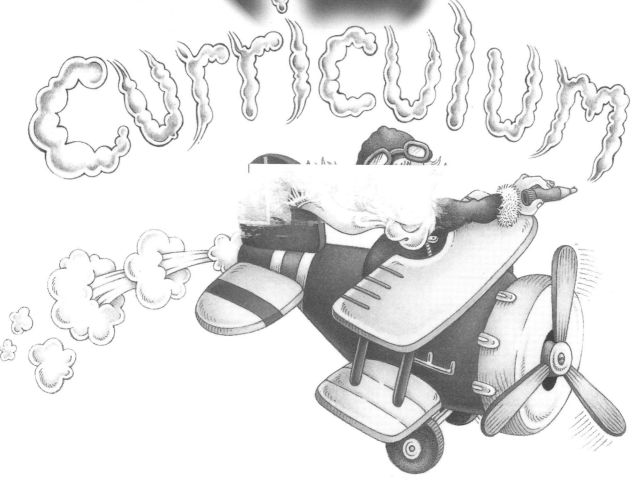

Clare White

Clare White gained her teaching qualification at Manchester. She has over ten years experience teaching children across the primary age group and has specialised in literacy and history.

As Acting Head, Clare has successfully led her last school out of Special Measures.

Contents

Published by
Hopscotch Educational Publishing Ltd
Unit 2
The Old Brushworks
56 Pickwick Road
Corsham
Wiltshire
SN13 9BX

01249 701701

© 2004 Hopscotch Educational Publishing

Written by Clare White
Series design by Blade Communications
Cover illustration by Susan Hutchison
Illustrated by Jane Bottomley and Sarah Wimperis
Printed by Colorman (Ireland) Ltd.

ISBN 1-904307-35-3

Clare White hereby asserts her moral right to be identified as the author of this work in accordance with the Copyright, Designs and Patents Act, 1988.

Introduction

About the series

Writing Across the Curriculum is a series of books aimed at developing and enriching the writing skills of children at Key Stage 2. Matched to the National Literacy Strategy's *Framework for Teaching* and the QCA's Schemes of Work, each book contains comprehensive lesson plans in two different subject areas for recount, report, instruction, explanation, persuasion and discussion (in Year 6) writing.

There are four books in the series: Year 3, Year 4, Year 5 and Year 6.

Each book aims to:

- support teachers by providing detailed lesson plans on how to incorporate the teaching of writing skills within different subject areas;

- develop teachers' confidence in using shared writing sessions by providing example scripts that the teachers can use or adapt;

- reduce teachers' preparation time through the provision of photocopiable resources;

- develop and enhance children's writing skills through stimulating and purposeful activities;

- encourage children's enjoyment of writing.

About each book

Each book is divided into separate chapters for each writing genre. Each chapter contains:

- an introductory page of teachers' notes that outlines the key structural and linguistic features and guidelines on the teaching and progression of that particular writing genre;

- two units of work, each on a different subject area.

Each unit of work is divided into four lesson plans that can be carried out over a period of time. These lessons are called:

'Switching on' – introduces the concepts;

'Revving up' – develops the concepts;

'Taking off' – instigates the planning stage of the writing;

'Flying solo' – encourages independent writing.

Each lesson plan is divided as follows:

- Learning objectives;

- Resources;

- What to do;

- Plenary.

Most lessons are supported by **photocopiable sheets**. Some of these sheets provide background information for the children and others provide support in the form of writing frames. Most lessons have an exemplar text that can be shared with the children. There is usually an annotated version of this text for the teacher. The annotated version points out the structural and linguistic features of the text. It should be noted, however, that only one example of each feature is provided and that the features are presented as a guide only.

Recount writing

What is a recount text?

A recount is quite simply a retelling of an event. The retelling can be used to impart information or to entertain the reader. Recounts can be personal (from the point of view of someone who was there) or impersonal.

Structural features

- Usually begins with an introduction to orientate the reader. Often answers the questions 'who?', 'what?', 'when?', 'where?' and 'why?'
- Main body of text then retells the events in chronological order
- Ends with a conclusion that briefly summarises the text or comments on the event

Linguistic features

- Past tense
- First person (personal recounts) or third person (impersonal)
- Focuses on named individuals or participants
- Uses time connectives to aid chronological order (firstly, afterwards, meanwhile, subsequently, finally)
- Often contains interesting details to bring incidents alive to the reader

Examples of recount texts

- newspaper reports
- diary entries
- letters
- write-up of trips or activities
- autobiographies/biographies

Teaching recount writing

At first glance, recounts seem to be relatively straightforward. After all, children seem to get plenty of practice doing their 'news' writing at school! However, as with any retelling, it is easy for children to neglect to include vital pieces of information. The knowledge of the event is in the children's heads and it is our job, as teachers, to make sure that that knowledge is shared with the reader in order to make the event purposeful for them. Children tend to list events, as if on a timeline, but they need to include specific information and use relevant connectives so that the reader is able to have all the information needed to imagine themselves there.

Many children need a lot of support in organising the information chronologically. A flow chart is a useful tool to enable children to sequence events in the correct order. It also enables them to see where there are natural divisions for paragraphs. A word bank of time connectives could also prove useful.

Encourage the children to organise the planning of their recount by listing information under the headings: who, what, when, where, why and how. This will ensure they include all the vital information.

Recount writing – progression

Simple recounts are introduced in Key Stage 1 (Reception: T15; Year 1, Term 3: T20).

In Year 3 children experiment with recounting the same event in a variety of ways, such as a story, a letter or a newspaper report (Term 3: T22).

In **Year 4** children examine opening sentences that set scenes and capture interest and identify the key features of newspapers (Term 1: T18, T20). They write newspaper style reports (Term 1: T24). They learn to make short notes (Term 2: T21).

In Year 5 (Term 1: T21, T23, T24, T26) children learn to identify the features of recounted texts such as sports reports and diaries and to write recounts based on subject, topic or personal experiences for different audiences. They discuss the purpose of note taking and how this influences the nature of the notes made.

In Year 6 (Term 1: T11, T14; Term 3: T19, T22) children are reading to distinguish between biography and autobiography and are developing the skills of biographical and autobiographical writing in role. They review a range of text features and select the appropriate style and form to suit a specific purpose and audience.

Unit 1

Lesson focus

History Unit 7 – Why did Henry VIII marry six times?

Overall aim

To analyse the main features of a recount and to write a recount about the wives of Henry VIII.

History emphasis

In this unit the children learn about the Tudor period of history and the reign of King Henry VIII. They develop skills of using written and pictorial sources to research his life, the political and religious reasons for his six marriages and the key events of his reign.

Literacy links

Year 4, Term 1: T16, T18, S2
Year 4, Term 2: T21

About this unit

This unit gives children the opportunity to write a recount text based on the story of Henry VIII's six marriages, focusing on the chronological order of events. They also develop speaking and listening skills through role play.

These lessons should ideally be taught towards the end of the history unit.

Switching on

Learning objectives

■ To read, enjoy and understand a recount text.

■ To identify the key structural and linguistic features of a recount text.

Resources

■ Sheets A, B and C (pages 10 to 13)

What to do

Begin the lesson by discussing what the children know of the Tudor king Henry VIII. Tell them that over the next few lessons they are going to find out about the special features of recount writing and then write their own recount about Henry VIII and his six wives.

Ask them to tell you what they think a recount is. Give them a few minutes to discuss this in pairs to share their ideas. Take a few suggestions and then agree that a recount is a piece of writing that retells events from either a personal or an impersonal point of view. Make sure the children understand the difference between personal (from the point of view of someone who was actually there) and impersonal (from the point of view of someone who was not actually there).

Next, show the class an enlarged copy of Sheet B. Read the text together. Then, without discussing it any further, tell the children that for their independent work they are going to begin identifying the special features of recount writing. Cover up the text.

Give out copies of Sheet C to mixed ability pairs of children. Tell them that the text on the puzzle page has been taken from the sheet they have just read together. Explain that you want them to read the three extracts and decide where in the text they come from – the beginning, the middle, or the end – and to give a reason why they think this.

Tell them that they should then go through each extract and make notes about and/or underline any features they notice about the text, such as the verb tense used, types of words used and how the text is set out. Agree a set time limit for this task, such as ten minutes.

As you circulate around the class, or sit working with a group, point the children in the right direction by asking questions such as:

'This extract is from the beginning of the text. What do you call the first paragraph of a text? Introduction – that's right. What is the purpose of this introduction?' (It is setting the scene, introducing the who, what, when, where and why of the text.)

'*What is the verb tense used?*' (The past tense.) '*Can you give me an example of a verb in the past tense from the extract? Why is the past tense used?*' (Because the events that are being retold have already happened.)

The first extract is in fact the conclusion of the recount. It makes the closing statements of the text, bringing the writing to a satisfactory ending. The conclusion uses good examples of past tense verbs; for example, 'had', 'ate' and 'died'.

The next extract is the introduction of the recount. It introduces King Henry VIII, the subject of the recount and provides the reader with a little background information about him, when he reigned and what he was famous for. The introduction is a good example of writing in the third person – an impersonal recount.

The last extract is a couple of the paragraphs from the middle of the recount. It illustrates the sequential organisation of the text, explaining what happened in time order. It uses time connectives to aid chronological sequence of the text.

It is a good example of using interesting details which bring the character of Henry to life.

Plenary

When you have called the children back together again, begin by asking for a volunteer to read the first extract on the 'Recount puzzle'. Then ask what special features they identified. Discuss their answers.

Uncover the enlarged text (Sheet B). Annotate it as the children give you their answers, highlighting the structural and linguistic features that they have identified. Work through all three extracts in this way. At the end, make sure all the key features of recount writing have been included. (You could compare their findings with Sheet A on page 10.)

Finish by telling the children that in the next lesson they will be gathering information about Henry VIII's six wives, ready for writing their own recount.

Revving up

Learning objectives

- To compile a timeline.
- To gather information about Henry VIII's six wives.
- To think up and ask questions.

Resources

- Sheet D (page 14), cut up into cards
- Sheet E (pages 15 and 16)
- 'Washing line' and pegs
- Ideally – Tudor costume and props such as a crown and throne

What to do

Tell the children that later in the lesson they will be having an unusual visitor. They will have the opportunity to ask the visitor questions to help them find information to use in their recount about Henry VIII. Tell them that their visitor knows a lot about Henry VIII and you will be putting all the information they get on a timeline.

Explain that first they need to think about the types of questions they could ask. To set the scene, give out the cards from Sheet D to six children and, together as a class, recap on who Henry VIII married and in which order. As you do so, ask the child with the relevant card to hang it on the washing line. This is a good opportunity to tell the children about the rhyme to help them remember what happened to each wife:

Divorced, beheaded, died,

Divorced, beheaded, survived.

The children still need to remember the wives' names and their order:

Catherine, Anne, Jane,

Anne, Catherine and Catherine.

As each card is hung up on the washing line, hold a brief discussion about the kind of questions the children could ask to gather their information about Henry and his wives. Prompt the children by thinking aloud and saying, for example, *'For how many years was Henry married to Catherine of Aragon?'*, *'I wonder why Henry beheaded Anne Boleyn?'*, *'What kind of person was Catherine Parr?'*, *'Was Henry marrying for love or to make an alliance for new land?'* and so on.

Then, send the children off in pairs to think up two or three questions to ask their visitor. (In order to make sure all Henry VIII's wives are covered, allocate different wives to different groups of children.) Tell them to write their questions down. Explain that when they meet their visitor they will be able to make notes about the answers.

The visitor
Arrange for another member of staff or a parent to pretend to be King Henry VIII. (Or take on this role yourself. If you are Henry you will be able to give the children all the information you require them to have for their recount.) Ideally, the character should be dressed for the part and stay in role – trying to throw themselves into the part!

Introduce yourself or the visitor to the children, perhaps requesting everyone to bow and curtsey! Then, the person in role as Henry VIII asks the children if they have any questions to ask him. Allow one question from each pair. The questions should be answered in role, giving the questioners time to jot down answers. The children should only make notes about their particular question – ready to add to the timeline in the next lesson. (Use Sheet E as a reference for information.)

Plenary

Round off the lesson by leading a discussion to recap the main points of information learned from King Henry VIII.

Ask the children open-ended questions such as:

'What did you think of King Henry VIII?'

'Did you learn anything new about his life?'

'What did you find most interesting about what he said?'

Tell the children that in the next lesson they will be writing up their notes on the information that they have learned from their 'meeting' with King Henry VIII.

Taking off

Learning objectives

■ To make brief notes on a timeline to plan a recount.

■ To plan and write the introduction to a recount.

■ To use structural and linguistic features of a recount.

Resources

■ Sheet A (page 10)

■ Blank cards, pegs

■ Washing line timeline from 'Revving up'

What to do

Tell the children that today they are going to begin to write their recount text. Explain that in order to do this, they need to do two things:

1. Make notes on the class timeline adding information learned from 'meeting' King Henry VIII;

2. Plan what they want to say in the introduction of their recount.

Ask the children to refer to their notes from the 'Revving up' lesson when they 'met' King Henry VIII. Read out the name of each wife, one at a time, and ask if anyone has any information about this marriage that you could add to the timeline. Listen to the answers and make notes in the past tense on a card. Add this card to the washing line timeline. Complete this activity for all six wives.

Next, draw five circles on the board. Write 'Who?', 'What?', 'Where?', 'When?' and 'Why?' in each of the circles. Tell the children that they are now going to plan their introductory paragraph.

Ask the children to tell you what they think the purpose of an introduction is. Take a few suggestions from them and agree that an introductory paragraph sets the scene for the reader. It introduces to the reader who the recount is about, when the events took place and where the events happened. It gives a basic outline of what the events were and it tries to get the reader interested so that they will read on! The 'Who?', 'What?', 'Where?', 'When?' and 'Why?' provide the reader with background information which orientates the reader and makes the subsequent text easier to follow.

Next, ask for suggestions from the children about what to write in your planning circles. Take each circle in turn and listen to several answers before making notes in the circles. Answers might include:

Who?	King Henry VIII of England, Henry Tudor
What?	married six times
Where?	England
When?	1509 – 1547
Why?	for love, to have a male heir, to make alliances for power, money or new land

Once all the circles are completed, ask the children to write their own introductory paragraphs to their recounts. Remind them of the linguistic and structural features of recount texts by displaying an enlarged version of Sheet A and going briefly through it with them again.

Plenary

Cover up Sheet A. Select three children, choosing a range of abilities, to read out their work. Praise each one for achieving a different aspect of an introduction, such as remembering to include 'Who?', 'What?', 'Where?', 'When?' and 'Why?' information, using the past tense, third person and so on. Ask the rest of the class to make a suggestion on how the work could be improved (with the owner's permission).

Finish the lesson by reading out the introduction from Sheet A, substituting the verbs for ones in the present and future tenses; for example, *'Henry Tudor will succeed to the throne of England in 1509.'* Reread the paragraph, sentence by sentence, asking for volunteers to identify the verbs and then change them to the past tense.

Flying solo

Learning objective

■ To write the main body of text and the conclusion of a recount.

Resources

■ Sheet A (page 10)

■ Washing line timeline from 'Taking off'

What to do

Tell the children they are now going to 'fly solo' and finish writing their own recount texts.

Look at the timeline together and ask the children to suggest to you the order of the information they will include in their recount (information about each of Henry's wives).

Ask *'What will the first paragraph after the introduction be about? That's right – Henry's first wife, Catherine of Aragon. Who can tell me something about Catherine of Aragon?'* Take a few answers; for example, *'Henry was married to her for 20 years. He divorced her because she did not manage to bear him a son and heir to the throne.'* Then ask *'How might we write this in sentences?'*

Remind the children of the work they did in 'Taking off' on verb tenses by showing them the following three sentences and asking which sentence is written in the correct tense for recount text writing.

King Henry VIII was married to his first wife, Catherine of Aragon, for 20 years.

King Henry VIII has been married to his first wife, Catherine of Aragon, for 20 years.

King Henry VIII will be married to his first wife, Catherine of Aragon, for 20 years.

Continue modelling the first few sentences of the first paragraph.

Send the children off to complete their own recounts. After ten minutes stop them and ask a few volunteers to read out a paragraph of their work so far. Highlight the good points and correct any misconceptions they may have.

Select a group to work with, either one requiring support or one requiring enrichment. For the group requiring support, allocate a different wife to each child. They should write their sentences for their own paragraph and then all the paragraphs could be joined together to make a finished recount. They could write the conclusion as a group effort.

For the group requiring enrichment, allow the children time to begin writing and then ask them to share their writing with you and the rest of the group. Highlight the good points and discuss as a group ways in which the writing could be improved. Give the children time to make these improvements to their work.

Plenary

Choose a recount text from a more able child to read out to the class. After you have read it once, ask the rest of the class to identify good points of the writing. Points to raise might include:

- Does the introduction include details of 'who', 'when', 'where', 'why' and 'what'?
- Are the key events arranged in paragraphs and in chronological order?
- Is it written in the past tense?
- Are linking words or phrases used to link sentences and paragraphs?
- Are time connectives used to aid the chronological order of who Henry married?

Then reread the text again, asking the rest of the class to raise their hands every time they hear a verb in the past tense.

An enjoyable way to finish off this series of lessons is by reading extracts from *Horrible Histories: The Terrible Tudors* by Terry Deary, published by Scholastic. While you are reading, the children could draw pictures of Henry VIII or any of his wives in order to complete their recount.

Henry VIII

title to say what the recount is about

Henry Tudor succeeded to the throne of England in 1509, after the death of his elder brother, Arthur. He was an impressive figure, six feet tall and keenly athletic. He reigned for nearly forty years, achieving a great many things, but he is perhaps most remembered for marrying six times.

introduction to set the scene – 'who', 'when', 'what', 'where' and 'why'.

named participants

The young prince Henry, the second son of Henry VII and Elizabeth of York, was born on 28th June 1491 at Greenwich. The royal Prince Henry is said to have had a very spoilt childhood. A story is told that he even had his own 'whipping boy' who was punished every time Henry did something wrong!

Henry was handsome, with auburn hair. He was a good athlete and loved jousting and hunting stags in the forests of England. He was also a talented student, and studied Latin, maths, astronomy, cosmology and music.

third person

Henry was famous for his love of music. He was a keen musician and composed many pieces of music, including a piece called 'Helas Madame'.

interesting details

Henry was a strong and decisive king: he knew what he wanted and generally got his own way even if it meant executing his enemies and indeed anyone who disagreed with him (including two of his wives!). When he became king the country was Catholic and was controlled by the Pope in Rome. When the Pope would not let Henry get divorced from his first wife, Catherine, Henry made himself head of the Church of England instead and subsequently gave himself the divorce he wanted.

time connective

Later in his reign, Henry closed all the monasteries and nunneries in England and took all the money from the monks and nuns. He threw them out onto the streets to beg and gave their monasteries to his friends for fine houses. This time in England was called the Reformation.

During his reign Henry started to build up the Navy into a strong fighting force. He loved his ships – he would often go and watch them being built and have parties on board. His most famous ship was the 'Mary Rose'. She was built in Portsmouth around 1510 and was named after his sister.

past tense

Most people remember who Henry VIII was because he had six wives. He married for different reasons: to have a male heir to succeed him to the throne, to make alliances with foreign countries and it is even said he married for love!

conclusion

By the end of his life, some historians say that Henry was a sad and lonely person. He was apparently terrified of getting ill, and anyone who had had contact with diseases such as smallpox or the plague was not allowed in court. He was overweight; he ate vast amounts of food and drank lots of wine and beer. He became so fat that he had to be carried everywhere by servants. He also had a bad leg, with ulcers possibly from an old jousting wound. On 28th January 1547 he died at Greenwich.

information organised in paragraphs in chronological order

Henry VIII

Henry Tudor succeeded to the throne of England in 1509, after the death of his

elder brother, Arthur. He was an impressive figure, six feet tall and keenly athletic. He reigned for nearly forty years, achieving a great many things, but he is perhaps most remembered for marrying six times.

The young prince Henry, the second son of Henry VII and Elizabeth of York, was born on 28th June 1491 at Greenwich. The royal Prince Henry is said to have had a very spoilt childhood. A story is told that he even had his own 'whipping boy' who was punished every time Henry did something wrong!

Henry as a boy

Henry was handsome, with auburn hair. He was a good athlete and loved jousting and hunting stags in the forests of England. He was also a talented student, and studied Latin, maths, astronomy, cosmology and music.

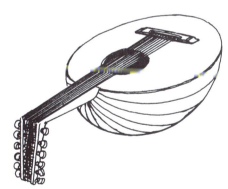

Henry played the lute

Henry was famous for his love of music. He was a keen musician and composed many pieces of music, including a piece called 'Helas Madame'.

Henry was a strong and decisive King: he knew what he wanted and generally got his own way even if it meant executing his enemies and indeed anyone who disagreed with him (including two of his wives!). When he became king the country was Catholic and was controlled by the Pope in Rome. When the Pope would not let Henry get divorced from his first wife, Catherine, Henry made himself head of the Church of England instead and subsequently gave himself the divorce he wanted.

Later in his reign, Henry closed all the monasteries and nunneries in England and took all the money from the monks and nuns. He threw them out onto the streets to beg and gave their monasteries to his friends for fine houses. This time in England was called the Reformation.

During his reign Henry started to build up the Navy into a strong fighting force. He loved his ships – he would often go and watch them being built and have parties on board. His most famous ship was the 'Mary Rose'. She was built in Portsmouth around 1510 and was named after his sister.

A Tudor ship

Most people remember who Henry VIII was because he had six wives. He married for different reasons: to have a male heir to succeed him to the throne, to make alliances with foreign countries and it is even said he married for love!

Henry as an old man

By the end of his life, some historians say that Henry was a sad and lonely person. He was apparently terrified of getting ill, and anyone who had had contact with diseases such as smallpox or the plague was not allowed in court. He was overweight; he ate vast amounts of food and drank lots of wine and beer. He became so fat that he had to be carried everywhere by servants. He also had a bad leg, with ulcers possibly from an old jousting wound. On 28th January 1547 he died at Greenwich.

Recount puzzle

Put these extracts from the text in the correct order. Find examples of verbs in the past tense, the use of the third person and some time connectives.

Extract 1

By the end of his life, some historians say that Henry was a sad and lonely person. He was apparently terrified of getting ill, and anyone who had had contact with diseases such as smallpox or the plague was not allowed in court. He was overweight; he ate vast amounts of food and drank lots of wine and beer. He became so fat that he had to be carried everywhere by servants. He also had a bad leg, with ulcers possibly from an old jousting wound. On 28th January 1547 he died at Greenwich.

Extract 2

Henry Tudor succeeded to the throne of England in 1509, after the death of his elder brother, Arthur. He was an impressive figure, six feet tall and keenly athletic. He reigned for nearly forty years, achieving a great many things, but he is perhaps most remembered for marrying six times.

Extract 3

Henry was famous for his love of music. He was a keen musician, and composed many pieces of music, including a piece called 'Helas Madame'.

Henry was a strong and decisive king: he knew what he wanted and generally got his own way even if it meant executing his enemies and indeed anyone who disagreed with him (including two of his wives!). When he became king the country was Catholic and was controlled by the Pope in Rome. When the Pope would not let Henry get divorced from his first wife, Catherine, Henry made himself head of the Church of England instead and subsequently gave himself the divorce he wanted.

The wives of Henry VIII

Catherine of Aragon

Anne Boleyn

Jane Seymour

Anne of Cleves

Catherine Howard

Catherine Parr

Henry VIII factsheet

Henry was born in 1491, the second son of King Henry VII and Elizabeth of York.

....

He was a member of the Tudor Royal Family.

....

He married six times: Catherine of Aragon, Anne Boleyn, Jane Seymour, Anne of Cleves, Catherine Howard and Catherine Parr.

....

He married Catherine of Aragon (widow of his brother, Arthur) in 1509 when he became King. She was 17 and Henry was only 12. She was older and wiser than him and often gave him advice on how to rule. She was a good and faithful wife for over twenty years. She had many children, but only one survived, Mary, who would later become queen. Henry divorced her in 1533, because he had fallen in love with Anne Boleyn and because of his desire for a male heir.

....

Henry fell in love with Anne Boleyn when she was one of the ladies in the queen's household in 1522. By 1526 he was trying to get divorced from Catherine so that he could marry Anne. The head of the Catholic Church, the Pope, wouldn't allow it, so eventually Henry broke away from the church in Rome and declared himself the head of a new Church of England. He granted himself a divorce.

....

He married Anne Boleyn in 1533 and later that year she gave birth to a girl, Elizabeth, who would grow up to be a strong queen for England.

....

Henry accused Anne Boleyn of infidelity, a treasonous charge for the king's consort. There is a letter from Anne begging Henry to believe in her innocence but he did not give in and in 1536 she was beheaded. Eleven days later Henry married this third wife.

....

He married Jane Seymour in 1536. She was from an old and noble family and was a gentle and modest girl. She died giving birth to Henry's only male heir, Edward. It is said that Henry loved Jane the best of all his wives and he waited two years before marrying again.

....

Henry decided to look all over Europe for a bride. He sent painters to paint any eligible brides so he could see what they looked like. After viewing Hans Holbein's beautiful portrait of the German princess Anne of Cleves he agreed to marry her early in 1540, without ever having met her!

....

When Anne arrived in England, Henry was very keen to meet her but she didn't speak any English and didn't know who he was. The meeting did not go very well. He is said to have not liked the way she looked and to have called her a horse! He couldn't break his promise to marry her but the marriage only lasted six months.

....

Catherine Howard, Henry's next wife, was a young cousin of Anne Boleyn. She has been described as lively, pretty and kind. However, she was previously secretly engaged to one man and possibly a second one too. When the king found out he had both the men's heads chopped off, followed by Catherine's in 1542.

....

Catherine Parr became his wife in 1543. She nursed him until his death in 1547.

Unit 2

Lesson focus

Religious Education Unit 4b – Celebrations: Christmas

Overall aim

To analyse the main features of a recount and to write a recount about Mary and Joseph's journey to Bethlehem and on to Egypt.

Religious Education emphasis

In this unit the children learn about the Christian story of Christmas through the theme of journeys.

Literacy links

Year 4, Term 1: T16, T18, S2
Year 4, Term 2: T21

About this unit

In this unit the children record the Christmas story through the theme of journeys, Mary and Joseph's journey to Bethlehem and then on to Egypt. Role play is used to give the children the opportunity to re-enact the journey and develop their knowledge of the sequence of events and their understanding of how Mary and Joseph may have felt on the journey.

Switching on

Learning objectives

■ To read, enjoy and understand a recount text.

■ To role play retelling the recount.

Resources

■ A children's Bible

■ Pictures of life in biblical times

■ An atlas

What to do

Tell or read the story of Mary and Joseph's journey from Nazareth to Bethlehem and then on to Egypt.

Explain to the children that they are going to write a recount of this journey, illustrated with a pictorial map. Tell them that in order to help them do this, they are going to imagine that they are Mary and Joseph travelling on their long journey.

Ask the children to tell you what they think it was like living in the time when Mary and Joseph did. What were the houses/clothes/roads like? What jobs did people do? Look at pictures in the children's Bible and any others that you have of the period. Ask them what they think life was like for Mary and Joseph.

Use an atlas to show them where Nazareth, the town of Bethlehem and the country of Egypt are. How long a journey did they have?

Ask the children to close their eyes and try to imagine the journey as you describe it. Divide the journey into sections (getting ready, the journey itself and arrival) and ask questions to help the children imagine what Mary and Joseph must have experienced. Questions could include:

Getting ready:
'How are you feeling?'
'What are you going to take with you?'
'Who do you say goodbye to?'
'Does anything about the journey worry you?'
'How long does it take you to prepare for the journey?'
'Who helps you?'

The journey itself:
'What do you see along the way?'
'Who do you meet?'
'What is it like travelling on the donkey?'
'How comfortable are you?'
'Where do you stop to eat and drink?'
'How are you feeling on the journey?'

The arrival at Bethlehem:
'It is late and getting cold, and you can't find anywhere to stay. How are you feeling?'

'What are you going to do?'

'What happens when you ask for accommodation?'

'Who eventually helps you?'

'What do you think of the stable?'

'Are you glad to be able to rest at last?'

Now, explain that they need to imagine that Jesus has been born and they have received all their visitors. Remind them that Joseph has a dream where an angel warns him that Jesus is in danger and that he must take Mary and the baby to Egypt where they will be safe. Ask the children to imagine how Mary and Joseph must have felt, having to leave quickly in the middle of the night.

Tell them that you now want them to prepare a role play about the story. Divide them into pairs or threes (to include the angel) and allocate a scene to each group to act out. Allow them sufficient time to discuss their roles and practise their scene.

Plenary

Ask each group to present their role play to the rest of the class. Choose a good example of role play from each scene and finish the lesson by watching these groups consecutively role playing Mary and Joseph's journey from Nazareth to Bethlehem and then on to Egypt.

Revving up

Learning objectives

■ To compile a timeline.

■ To identify the key structural and linguistic features of a recount.

■ To draw a pictorial map.

Resources

■ Sheet B (pages 23 and 24)

■ Sheet C (page 25) cut into speech bubbles

■ Sheet D (page 26) cut into cards

■ Blank cards, sticky-tack, washing line, pegs

What to do

Begin the lesson by telling the children that you have a text detailing the journey made by the Wise Men to visit the baby Jesus. Display an enlarged version of Sheet B.

Ask the children to read it quietly to themselves first. Then ask for a volunteer to read the first paragraph and continue by choosing different children to read each of the remaining paragraphs. Discuss what happens in the text by asking the children to recall the journey in sequence.

Tell them that they are now going to identify the special features of recount writing and make a display of these features to help them write their own recounts later on.

Display the three large bubbles that outline the structural features of the text on Sheet C; that is:

Introduction – setting the scene – who? what? where? why? when?

Sequential organisation – what happened, in time order

Conclusion – closing sentences to bring the writing to an end

Read the three bubbles with the children, making sure they understand each feature. Ask for a volunteer to sticky-tack a bubble beside an example of that feature in the enlarged text. Revisit the meaning of each feature as you do so; for example, in the introduction the 'who' are the three Wise Men, the 'where' is a country far away from Bethlehem, the 'when' is soon after Jesus was born, the 'why' is because they knew it was something special and the 'what' is the Wise Men seeing a new star telling them a new ruler had been born.

Tell the children that they are now going to remind themselves of the journey made by Mary and Joseph from Nazareth to Bethlehem and then on to Egypt. Give out the cards from Sheet D to individual children. Ask them to organise themselves into an appropriate order, to show a timeline of the journey. Read through the cards with the rest of the class to agree that they are in the correct sequence.

Then, ask the children to suggest details about the journey to add to the timeline. Write their suggestions, in the past tense, on pieces of card and ask volunteers to hold these cards and stand in the timeline. For example, a note to accompany the card about Mary and Joseph arriving in Bethlehem might read 'middle of the night, inns all full, Mary exhausted'. Peg the cards up on a washing line as a reference for the children.

Explain that they are now going to draw a map sequencing the events of Mary and Joseph's journey from Nazareth to Bethlehem and then on to Egypt. The map is a type of timeline and you want them to label the events on the map, adding detailed notes.

Plenary

Share some of the children's maps. Discuss ideas for improvements and additions.

Finish by referring again to Sheet B. Remind them about the structural feature bubbles and ask them to tell you anything else they notice about the language of the text. Take two or three suggestions and then show the children the linguistic features described in the remaining bubbles from Sheet C. Ask for a volunteer to sticky-tack each feature bubble by an example of the feature in the text. Discuss the meaning of each feature as you do this.

Taking off

Learning objectives

■ To revise the meaning of verbs.

■ To improve a recount by adding more powerful verbs.

Resources

■ An enlarged copy of Sheet B (pages 23 and 24)

■ Thesauruses

What to do

Begin the lesson by revising what verbs are. Ask the children to give you examples of verbs and write these on the board.

Then write the following sentence on the board.

The horse jumped over the fence.

Ask the children to identify the verb (jumped). Explain that the word 'jumped' is quite a boring verb. Ask *'Can you think of a more exciting one to use to make the sentence more interesting?'* Take two or three suggestions and write these on the board. Remind them about using a thesaurus to find other words. Look up the word 'jump' and add other words to the list. Reread the sentences using these verbs. Do they think the sentence sounds more interesting?

Display the enlarged version of Sheet B. Read the first few paragraphs aloud, asking volunteers to circle the verbs and then suggest more powerful alternatives. For example, can they find better verbs for 'saw' in the first paragraph? Is there a better verb than 'said' in the fifth paragraph?

Give the children copies of Sheet B and ask them to do the same with the rest of the text, working with a partner. Tell them that you want them to circle the verbs in pencil and then think of more powerful verbs to replace them and to write the new verb in over the top of the old one. Remind them to use a thesaurus to help them.

As the children are doing this, sit with each pair in turn, making sure they can identify the verbs and can make useful alternative suggestions.

Plenary

Finish by asking for a couple of volunteers to read out their paragraphs of the texts with the new verbs. (Enlarged copies of their text or OHP copies would be useful for the rest of the class to see.)

Ask the rest of the class to respond positively to the work, discussing the verbs chosen.

Flying solo

Learning objective

■ To write a recount.

Resources

■ Sheet A (page 22)

■ Washing line timeline from 'Revving up'

■ Maps from 'Revving up'

What to do

Tell the children that they are going to do some shared writing of a recount using the timeline and pictorial map they made of Mary and Joseph's journey in the 'Revving up' lesson. They may also like to refer to their map to help sequence the events on the journey.

Begin by discussing who the audience might be – other classes in the school or a display board, perhaps. Display an enlarged version of Sheet A, reminding the children of all the special features that need to be included in a recount. Now say, 'I am ready to begin writing my introduction.'

Begin to write in front of them, remembering to model gathering your ideas, rehearsing the sentence and reading back, paying attention to vocabulary choices. The following is a script for your eyes only which you can use or adapt. The text in italics is what you say out loud as if to yourself; the text in bold is what you write.

> *Right, what does an introduction do? That's right – it sets the scene; it's the who, what, when, why and where. So the 'who' is Mary and Joseph, the 'where' is Nazareth, the 'when' is a long time ago and the 'what' is they are going on a journey to Bethlehem.* **Mary and Joseph lived happily together in Nazareth, a village in the hills of Galilee. They were looking forward to the birth of the baby Mary was expecting. The Roman Emperor Augustus made a new law.** *I'll just read that back. I think I need to tell the reader why the emperor made a new law, so I'll add…* **The Roman Emperor Augustus, who ruled the whole country, made a new law saying that everyone must go to the town their family came from to register so they could be taxed. Joseph's family had come from Bethlehem so he had to go back there.**
>
> *Now, one of the features of recount writing is words that engage the reader, so I need to use more interesting verbs and adjectives. So let's rewrite that last sentence adding adjectives.* **Joseph's family had come from Bethlehem, so he had to make the long and tiring journey back there with Mary.**

Move on to discuss the next paragraph. Refer to the timeline and ask the children what the next paragraph should be about. Then ask them to write their recounts up to, but not including, the conclusion.

During the independent work, sit with a group of children to support and extend their writing through questioning and reference to the special features of recount texts.

When they are ready, ask the children to tell you the purpose of the last paragraph in a recount (the conclusion). Ask 'What can you tell me about the ending of the journey that Mary and Joseph made?' Take a few suggestions and then ask them to work in pairs to think of a couple of sentences to conclude their recount, writing on dry whiteboards, perhaps.

Plenary

Ask for volunteers to read out their conclusions. Pick out the good points from each conclusion and discuss them with the rest of the class.

Give them time to add their conclusions to their recounts, making any changes they wish to.

Finally, consider once again the special features of recount writing. Points to discuss might include:

A good introduction – the who? what? where? when? and why? setting the scene;

The use of paragraphs to help sequence the events;

The use of time connectives (firstly, afterwards, meanwhile, subsequently, finally);

Interesting examples of powerful verbs.

Ask the children if they would have done anything differently if they were starting their recount again. Give them a couple of minutes in pairs to reflect on their own work, picking out one good point and something they would do differently if starting their recount again.

The Wise Men

title to say what the recount is about

third person

named participants

interesting details

time connective

conclusion

introduction to set the scene – 'who', 'when', 'what', 'where' and 'why'

information organised in paragraphs in chronological order

past tense

A long way from Bethlehem, in another country, lived three Wise Men who studied the stars. One night shortly after Jesus was born, they were gazing into the clear night sky when they saw a new star shining out. It was bigger and brighter than any other star they had seen. After consulting their books and charts, they realised that this new star signified that a new ruler had been born. They decided to go on a journey to find him.

The Wise Men began their long journey, carrying gifts with them for the new baby. They knew which road to take because the star moved brightly across the night sky ahead of them. At last they arrived in the city of Jerusalem.

There, they asked the people, 'Where can we find the new baby? We have seen his star in the sky and we know he is born to be the king of the Jews.'

King Herod heard that three Wise Men were trying to find a new baby, who they said was going to be the king of the Jews. This made King Herod very angry, but also a little frightened. The Roman rulers of the country had made him the king of the Jews. He asked his priests what the Wise Men could mean. The priests looked at the old books and told Herod that, a long, long time ago, it had been prophesied that the king of the Jews would be born in Bethlehem.

Herod wanted to meet the Wise Men. At their meeting he told them to continue their journey and go to Bethlehem to find the baby. 'When you find the baby, tell me,' he said, 'so that I can visit him bearing gifts as well.' The Wise Men continued their journey along the road to Bethlehem. The star still moved ahead of them and then it seemed to stop right over the town. The Wise Men realised they had found the baby.

They found the baby in a stable with his mother and father, Mary and Joseph. When they saw baby Jesus the Wise Men knelt down in front of him and gave Mary the gifts they had brought with them; gold, frankincense and an ointment called myrrh. Then the Wise Men slipped away again into the night.

Finally, they began their journey home, travelling first to King Herod in Jerusalem. On the way they rested just outside Bethlehem. That night they had a dream. In the dream an angel warned them that Herod planned to harm the baby Jesus. When the Wise Men awoke in the morning, they decided to go home a different way so as not to see King Herod. They loaded up their camels and set off for home.

The Wise Men

A long way from Bethlehem, in another country, lived three Wise Men who studied the stars. One night shortly after Jesus was born, they were gazing into the clear night sky when they saw a new star shining out. It was bigger and brighter than any other star they had seen. After consulting their books and charts, they realised that this new star signified that a new ruler had been born. They decided to go on a journey to find him.

The Wise Men began their long journey, carrying gifts with them for the new baby. They knew which road to take because the star moved brightly across the night sky ahead of them. At last they arrived in the city of Jerusalem.

There, they asked the people, 'Where can we find the new baby? We have seen his star in the sky and we know he is born to be the king of the Jews.'

King Herod heard that three Wise Men were trying to find a new baby, who they said was going to be the king of the Jews. This made King Herod very angry, but also a little frightened. The Roman rulers of the country had made him the king of the Jews. He asked his priests what the Wise Men could mean. The priests looked at the old books and told Herod that, a long, long time ago, it had been prophesied that the king of the Jews would be born in Bethlehem.

Writing across the Curriculum

Herod wanted to meet the Wise Men. At their meeting he told them to continue their journey and go to Bethlehem to find the baby. 'When you find the baby, tell me,' he said, 'so that I can visit him bearing gifts as well.' The Wise Men continued their journey along the road to Bethlehem. The star still moved ahead of them and then it seemed to stop right over the town. The Wise Men realised they had found the baby.

They found the baby in a stable with his mother and father, Mary and Joseph. When they saw baby Jesus the Wise Men knelt down in front of him and gave Mary the gifts they had brought with them; gold, frankincense and an ointment called myrrh. Then the Wise Men slipped away again into the night.

Finally, they began their journey home, travelling first to King Herod in Jerusalem. On the way they rested just outside Bethlehem. That night they had a dream. In the dream an angel warned them that Herod planned to harm the baby Jesus. When the Wise Men awoke in the morning, they decided to go home a different way so as not to see King Herod. They loaded up their camels and set off for home.

Sheet C

introduction

*setting the scene –
who? what?
where? why?
when?*

**sequential
organisation**

*what happened,
in time order*

conclusion

*closing sentences
to bring the
writing to an end*

*written in the
past tense*

time connectives

*firstly, afterwards,
meanwhile,
subsequently, finally*

*third person
writing*

named people

*interesting
adjectives and
verbs*

The journey

The Roman Emperor Augustus made a new law stating that everyone must go to the town their family came from to register so that they could be taxed.

Joseph's family came from Bethlehem, so he and Mary loaded up their donkey and travelled to Bethlehem.

They arrived late in Bethlehem and the only room they could find was a stable. That night, the baby Jesus was born.

Shepherds from the fields outside Bethlehem visited the baby Jesus, after seeing a host of angels. Three Wise Men followed a bright star from a country far away to bring gifts to the baby Jesus.

After the Wise Men had left, Joseph had a dream. An angel warned him that Jesus was in danger and that he must take Mary and the baby to Egypt.

Mary and Joseph lived safely in Egypt with Jesus. Later, they returned to Nazareth when they knew King Herod was dead.

Report writing

What is a report text?

A report is a non-chronological text written to describe or classify something. It brings together a set of related information and sorts it into paragraphs of closely connected facts. Reports can also be used to compare and contrast.

Structural features

- Usually begins with an introduction to orientate the reader. Tells us 'who', 'what', 'where' and 'when'

- Main body of text is organised into paragraphs describing particular aspects of the subject

- Ends with a conclusion that briefly summarises the text

- Non-chronological

Linguistic features

- Often written in the present tense (except for historical reports)

- Usually uses generic nouns and pronouns (such as people, cats, buildings) rather than specific ones

- Written in an impersonal third person style

- Factual writing, often using technical words

- Language is used to describe and differentiate

- Linking words and phrases are used

- Occasional use of the passive

Examples of report texts

- non-fiction books
- newspaper/magazine articles
- school projects
- tourist guidebooks
- information leaflets

Teaching report writing

Writing a non-chronological report is a bit like collecting shells on the beach in a bucket and then sorting them into piles of similar shells, discarding anything that is damaged or has been scooped up that isn't a shell!

Children need to learn to gather from research relevant information about the subject they are going to describe, sort the information into groups of facts that go together and then link them in a logical order both within the paragraphs and between the paragraphs. They have to learn how to 'file' information into these paragraphs so that the reader can access the information easily and logically. Using sub-headings for paragraphs can help children organise their information. They need to choose which information is most important to the reader and elaborate on it.

One of the difficulties for children is to be able to research the information they need without simply copying out (or printing out) passages from reference sources. They need to be taught how to select key words and phrases and use them in their own sentences.

Report writing – progression

Simple non-chronological reports are introduced in Key Stage 1 (Year 1 – Term 2: T25; Year 2 – Term 3: T21).

In Year 3 children locate information in non-fiction books using the text structures – contents, index, headings, subheadings, page numbers and bibliographies. They record information from texts and write simple non chronological reports for a known audience (Term 1: T17, T18, T21, T22).

In **Year 4** children identify different types of text and different features of non-fiction texts in print and IT (Term 1: T16, T17) and they write non-chronological reports, including the use of organisational devices (Term 1: T21).

In Year 5 (Term 1: T26; Term 2: T22) children learn to make notes for different purposes and to plan, compose, edit and refine short non-chronological texts.

In Year 6 (Term 1: T17; Term 3: T19, T22) children are moving on to writing non-chronological reports linked to other subjects. They review a range of text features and select the appropriate style and form to suit a specific purpose and audience.

Unit 1

Lesson focus

Science Unit 4a – Moving and growing

Overall aim

To analyse the main features of non-chronological report writing and to write a report on movement.

Science emphasis

In this unit the children learn about how humans move. Using an ICT source, they gather information about three functions of the skeleton – protection, movement and support, and how muscles and joints allow movement. They also find out about how to stay healthy through eating a healthy diet, exercising and resting regularly and avoiding health risks such as smoking and drugs.

Literacy links

Year 4, Term 1: T16, T17, T27, S2

About this unit

In this unit the children are writing a non-comparative report describing how the human body moves. ICT is used to provide a source of information and the children record their notes on a spidergram.

This unit builds upon Science Unit 2A 'Health and growth' and Unit 3A 'Teeth and eating'. Children need to know scientific vocabulary for some parts of their body and to be able to use standard measurements for length. It links to knowledge and understanding of fitness and health in PE and leads to more complex work in Science Unit 5A 'Keeping healthy'.

Switching on

Learning objective

■ To read information texts about 'movement' and make simple notes.

Resources

■ Internet access

■ An IT text on 'movement'; for example, as contained within *http://www.learn.co.uk* or *http://www.bbc.co.uk/schools/revisewise*

■ A big non-fiction book (on any science topic)

What to do

Remind the children about the work they have been doing in science on moving and growing. Explain that they are going to research some facts on the internet and then write a report about movement using the information they have found.

Ask them to sit in pairs and tell their partner what they already know about how humans move. After a few minutes, ask a couple of children to tell the class what they already knew and what they have learned from their partner. Explain that they are now going to find out more.

Remind the children how to find information in non-fiction books by sharing the big book on science. Show them the contents and index pages. Ask how they help us find information. Ask them what other features they might find in the book that would help them to find things. Share ideas about the use of headings, subheadings, labelled diagrams and a glossary. Involve the children in locating some of the features they have suggested.

Explain that finding information on a website is very similar to using an information book. Tell them that the reader of an ICT text must also first locate the relevant pages they require. Demonstrate this by using *www.learn.co.uk* (or use similar ideas with another web site of your own choice).

If using *www.learn.co.uk*, do the following:

1. After the website has opened, click on 'enter learn.co.uk here'.

2. Think aloud as you navigate the site in order to explain the strategies you are using. For example, *'I am scanning the page to find the Science Key Stage 2 category'* [click on that] *'and then I need to locate pages on moving and growing'*. Scan down the list until you come to 'Movement'. Rest the curser on the word 'movement' and ask the children why they think it is written in a different colour and is underlined. (This is hypertext. It links the reader to other texts or parts of the same text, similar to an index in a book.) [Click on 'Movement'.]

3. Read through the facts on skeletons. Ask the children to suggest which words might be the key words. Point out the words in red and highlight them on the screen. Show them how to click on the underlined words to find out the meaning of the words. Compare this with a glossary in a book. Write on the board notes about the three functions of a skeleton.

4. Ask the children to find the key words in the 'bones' text. Share ideas about writing notes about these facts.

5. Scan down the list of the other units on the left of the screen. Where would we find information about muscles and movement? [Click on the sub-unit.] Read through some of the facts, explaining that to find all the information you have to scroll down the page.

6. Try out the diagrams by clicking on 'start' and 'reset'. How does this help the reader? How does this facility compare with a paper-based text? (It is interactive, provides commentaries and so on.)

Tell the children that you want them to continue using this website to find more information about movement, ready to write their report. Depending upon the resources available to you, either ask the children to work in pairs and continue looking at this website to make notes, or print off pages from the website and, still in pairs, they can read through the information, highlighting key words and phrases and record information in note form.

Plenary

Ask the pairs of children to join into groups of four. Give them five minutes to compare their information. Ask each group to feed back two or three facts they have found out to the class.

Discuss the work they have completed using ICT, comparing ICT with using books or leaflets to find information. Click on 'Let's recap' in *www.learn.co.uk* to revise the facts explored.

Collect the notes from the children. Write out sentences from these notes on separate strips of paper containing information about the skeleton, muscles, joints and tendons and ligaments. (This will be used in the 'Taking off' lesson.)

Revving up

Learning objectives

■ To identify the key structural and linguistic features of a non-chronological report.

■ To write a checklist for report writing.

Resources

■ Sheets A and B (pages 33 and 34)

What to do

Tell the children that they are now going to look at a particular non-fiction text type – a non-chronological report – to help them write their own report on 'movement' later on. Ask them to tell you what they think a report is and how it might be written and organised. Accept a couple of suggestions (for example, title, paragraphs, general opening and present tense) and then say, *'Let's look at a report to see if you are right!'* Display an enlarged version of Sheet B. Also display a blank spidergram and write 'healthy living' in the middle of the page (see below).

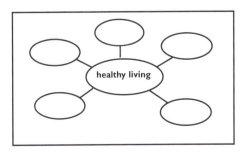

Decide together what the immediate features are that the children can see before they start to read (title, pictures and paragraphs). Read the opening paragraph and discuss its purpose. (Its purpose is to introduce the subject which is going to be described.) Begin to create a checklist of the features of report writing.

Ask for a volunteer to read the next two paragraphs straight through.

Agree with the children that both paragraphs continue to tell the reader about healthy living but ask them why there are two paragraphs and whether there is a difference between them. When they have concluded that each paragraph is about a different aspect of healthy living, suggest writing the subject of each paragraph in two ovals on the spidergram ('food' in one and 'exercise' in another). Tell the children that you will complete this spidergram in the plenary session. Continue the checklist.

Read paragraph 3 again. Stop at the end of the first sentence and ask the children to think up a question about the sentence (so that you can establish that they have understood the text). For example, *'Can you give three reasons why exercise keeps you healthy?'*

Investigate collectively the linguistic features used in the first three paragraphs, continuing the checklist; for example, a report describes the way things are, it is written in the present tense, each paragraph could have a subheading and it uses technical vocabulary such as 'carbohydrates' and 'muscles'.

Then move on to demonstrate how to gather the main points of paragraph 4 quickly. Read the first sentence and underline the main phrase or words – 'health risks', 'smoking', 'alcohol' and 'drugs'. Then in the next sentence, underline 'smoking', 'heart attacks', 'lung cancer' and 'breathing'. Similarly, underline the main points of the last sentence.

Continue by reading through to the end of the report. After reading the final paragraph ask the children what they would suggest might be the particular purpose of a closing paragraph and write it on the checklist.

Investigate collectively the linguistic features used in the last three paragraphs and add any further features to the checklist for report writing.

For their independent work, provide each pair of children with their own copy of the report text (Sheet B). Ask them to read and underline key words and/or phrases in

the same way as you have just done as a class. Then ask them to put the themes of each paragraph on a blank spidergram of their own.

Plenary

Ask for volunteers to describe the theme and main points of each paragraph of the report. Demonstrate filling in the class spidergram as the children give their feedback. Add 'smoking', 'alcohol' and 'drugs' in the other three ovals. Add brief notes around these ovals, such as 'carbohydrates', 'fats', 'proteins', 'vitamins', 'fibre' and 'water' around the word 'food' (see below). Points to make in general include: making concise notes, not too much detail on the spidergram, using technical language and so on.

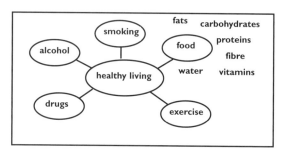

To finish the lesson, refer back to the checklist you have created on report writing. Ask the children, *'Have you spotted any other linguistic features during your reading of the report?'* Share their ideas. Show an enlarged version of the report (Sheet A). Go through all the features that are listed. Add any missing ones to the class list. Ask, *'How does a report compare to other non-fiction text types?'*

Taking off

Learning objectives

- To create a class spidergram on 'movement', using information gathered from the 'Switching on' lesson (using the *www.learn.co.uk* site).

- To write the introduction and first paragraph of their own report on 'movement'.

Resources

- Four large ovals with words such as 'skeleton', 'muscles', 'joints' and 'tendons and ligaments' written inside

- Sentence strips of facts gathered from 'Switching on'

- Checklist for report writing from 'Revving up'

What to do

Tell the children that they are now going to use what they have learned from the previous lesson to help them write their own report about movement. Remind them of the ICT research they did in the 'Switching on' lesson.

Show them an enlarged version of the spidergram below and explain that the ovals represent the main sections in the ICT text on movement.

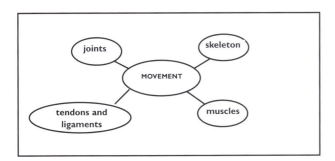

Position the four large ovals around the classroom and hand out a sentence strip to each child. Explain that each word in the ovals represents a different paragraph heading. Tell them that you have written out some facts from the lesson and that you want them to read their sentence and decide which circle it belongs to. Ask four to eight children at a time to come out and place their sentence near the circle they have chosen. When all the children have placed their sentences, look at each 'paragraph' and decide together if each sentence belongs in the chosen place. Do you need to add any extra paragraphs?

Explain that now you are going to show them how to write an introductory paragraph to a report and that, when they work on their own, they will be writing their own introductions and then the first paragraph of their 'movement' report.

Tell the children that in an introduction they have to introduce their subject and then make some general points which will be elaborated on in the paragraphs. Take two or three suggestions from them and then write your own introductory sentences; for example:

The skeleton is related to movement and support in humans. Muscles and joints in the human body work together to allow movement.

Talk through the rest of the introduction, encouraging the children to help with forming the ideas and constructing the sentences.

Then, ask the children what they think the second paragraph should be about. (Skeletons.) *'What information is going to be reported in this paragraph?'* (The reasons you have a skeleton, how many bones you have, what bones are like, the main bones in the human body and their function and so on.)

Make sure they can all see the displayed spidergram for 'MOVEMENT' and then send them off to write their own introduction and first paragraph.

Plenary

Ask several children to read out their introductions and first paragraphs. Discuss them as a class and then give the children a few moments to make notes on their own work of any changes they would like to make. Points to discuss could include *'Have you written in the correct verb tense?'* and *'Have you used any technical words?'*

Display the report checklist compiled in 'Revving up' for reference by the children.

Finish by discussing an appropriate order for the paragraphs in the rest of the report which they will be writing in the next lesson, using the spidergram as a prompt.

Flying solo

Learning objective

■ To write the next paragraphs and conclusion of their report on 'movement'.

Resources

■ The spidergram on 'MOVEMENT'

■ A checklist for report writing

What to do

Display the class spidergram on 'MOVEMENT' and the checklist for writing a report.

To set the children off on the right track, demonstrate the writing of the next paragraph on muscles, talking through the process of composing and revising sentences in the head. For example:

In order for the skeleton to move it needs muscles. Humans have over 600 different muscles in the body.

Ask the children to read through their introduction and first paragraph to refresh their memories about the report. Remind them that they have already decided which order to write the paragraphs in and point to the

next paragraph to be written. Ask them to begin writing the rest of their report on 'movement'.

After ten minutes or so, demonstrate the writing of the conclusion, talking through the process of composing and revising sentences. Ask the children, *'What is the function of a conclusion?'* (To repeat the most important points and perhaps emphasise a point of particular interest.) Ask them to look at their introductions to see what the main point of their report is. Take two or three suggestions and then write your own concluding sentences; for example:

So you can see that the human body has a very complicated system of bones, muscles, joints, tendons and ligaments that allow the body to move. Without such a system, humans would be unable to do the many things they can do, such as walking, running, climbing, talking and writing.

Ask the children to finish writing their paragraphs and then to write the conclusions for their reports. Diagrams could be added to the report as a homework project.

Plenary

Ask the children to work in pairs to read their reports to each other and to make suggestions for improvement. Make this a short activity. Bring the class back together again and share their ideas for making improvements. How confident do they now feel in being able to write a report? What advice could they give to others?

title
to say what the report is about

general nouns and pronouns

non-chronological organisation

present tense

conclusion to sum up

introduction to orientate the reader

information organised in paragraphs

third person

technical words

Healthy living

To stay healthy, humans need to do four things: eat sensibly, take exercise, rest regularly and make sensible choices about what they do to their bodies.

Humans, like all animals, need food. In order to remain healthy, a balanced diet is necessary and should contain carbohydrates, fats, proteins, minerals and vitamins, fibre and water.

Carbohydrates and fats are needed for energy. Carbohydrates can be found in bread, pasta, potatoes and biscuits, while cheese and butter provide the body with fats. Proteins help cells grow and repair. Fish, meat, milk and eggs are good sources of proteins. Foods that have vitamins and minerals include fruit and vegetables and they help the development of healthy cells. Bran, cereals, wholegrain bread, fruit and vegetables provide the body with fibre, which helps the food to move through the gut. 70% of the body is made up of water which comes mainly from drinks such as fruit juices.

Exercise is important for a healthy body. Exercise strengthens the muscles and develops the lungs. It helps body coordination develop so humans can throw and catch, for example. The body uses up food for energy and this helps prevent people from getting fat.

Taking health risks such as, smoking, drinking alcohol and taking drugs can damage the body. Smoking causes heart attacks, lung cancer and breathing problems. Tobacco contains nicotine, which is addictive.

Drinking alcohol in small amounts is not as harmful as smoking but it does slow down the body's reactions. Heavy drinking damages the liver, heart and stomach.

Drugs can be extremely dangerous if they are misused. Many are addictive and can cause damage to the brain.

So, to stay healthy, humans need to eat the right foods, keep well clear of dangerous drugs, know that smoking and drinking damage the body, do plenty of exercise and get enough rest.

Healthy living

To stay healthy, humans need to do four things: eat sensibly, take exercise, rest regularly and make sensible choices about what they do to their bodies.

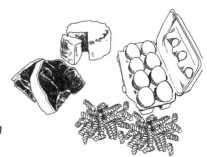

Humans, like all animals, need food. In order to remain healthy, a balanced diet is necessary and should contain carbohydrates, fats, proteins, minerals and vitamins, fibre and water.

Carbohydrates and fats are needed for energy. Carbohydrates can be found in bread, pasta, potatoes and biscuits, while cheese and butter provide the body with fats. Proteins help cells grow and repair. Fish, meat, milk and eggs are good sources of proteins. Foods that have vitamins and minerals include fruit and vegetables and they help the development of healthy cells. Bran, cereals, wholegrain bread, fruit and vegetables provide the body with fibre, which helps the food to move through the gut. 70% of the body is made up of water which comes mainly from drinks such as fruit juices.

Exercise is important for a healthy body. Exercise strengthens the muscles and develops the lungs. It helps body coordination develop so humans can throw and catch, for example. The body uses up food for energy and this helps prevent people from getting fat.

Taking health risks such as smoking, drinking alcohol and taking drugs can damage the body. Smoking causes heart attacks, lung cancer and breathing problems. Tobacco contains nicotine, which is addictive.

Drinking alcohol in small amounts is not as harmful as smoking but it does slow down the body's reactions. Heavy drinking damages the liver, heart and stomach.

Drugs can be extremely dangerous if they are misused. Many are addictive and can cause damage to the brain.

So, to stay healthy, humans need to eat the right foods, keep well clear of dangerous drugs, know that smoking and drinking damage the body, do plenty of exercise and get enough rest.

Unit 2

Lesson focus

Religious Education Unit 4d – Religions represented in the neighbourhood

Overall aim

To analyse the main features of a non-chronological report and to write a report about one of the religions represented in their local area.

Religious Education emphasis

In this unit the children find out about the leader, place of worship, beliefs, symbols and holy book of a religion that is represented in their local area by collecting and interpreting evidence from a range of sources.

Literacy links

Year 4, Term 1: T16, T17, T27, S2

About this unit

This unit gives the children the opportunity to record their learning in a report text based on a description of the characteristics and the lifestyle of a religion.

It draws together materials studied in all the units in Key Stage 1, in particular Unit 1D 'Beliefs and practice' and Unit 3A 'What do signs and symbols mean in religion?'

The lessons should be completed after the children have already found out about the religions in their area.

Switching on

Learning objectives

- To read, enjoy and understand a report text on Sikhism.
- To make a simple record of the information presented in a grid.

Resources

- Sheet B (pages 42 and 43)
- Sheet C (page 44)
- Large labels (or sticky notes) with the words 'leader', 'place of worship', 'beliefs', 'symbols' and 'holy book' written on them
- Reference sources about religions represented in the local area

What to do

Before this lesson, the children should have already found out about the different religions represented in their local area in the RE lessons. A display showing a range of artefacts from the different religions for the children to look at and handle would be useful.

To get the discussion started, ask the children to spend a few minutes talking to the child sitting next to them about what they have found out about the different religions in the neighbourhood. Then ask each pair to tell the rest of the class a couple of things they have remembered.

Discuss the places they have visited and the different people they have met, as well as the main features of each religion. Make a note on the board of each of the religions represented in the local area as the children mention them.

Explain to the class that over the next few lessons they are going to learn about the special features of report writing in order to write a group report about one of the religions in their area. Tell them that they will also be learning how to plan their report so they can write it successfully. Explain that they will then be presenting their report to another class or in assembly and that the reports will be compiled to make a class book, entitled 'Religions in our Neighbourhood'.

Explain that they are now going to read a report about Sikhism. Display an enlarged copy of Sheet B. Read the text aloud to the class, occasionally pretending not to understand the meaning of some words and demonstrating the strategies you would use to help you try and make sense of the text. For example, when you come to an 'unknown' word ask:

'Do you know any other words like this one?'

'Can we work it out from the other words in the text?' (context)

'What type of word is it?' (verb, noun and so on.)

'What do you think it means?'

'Let's look the word up in a dictionary.'

Now, focus closely on the way the text is organised. Explain that the first paragraph is called an introduction – it sets the scene – and the last paragraph is called a conclusion. Say that each of the paragraphs in between is about a different aspect of Sikhism. Show them the cut out labels with the words 'leader', 'place of worship', 'beliefs', 'symbols' and 'holy book' on them. Explain that these words summarise the purpose of the paragraphs. Hold up one at a time and ask for volunteers to match a paragraph to each one. Are there some paragraphs (apart from the introduction and the conclusion) that do not have a label? What label could we give it or them?

Tell the children that these labels will help to make up a recording grid. Begin by showing them a blank copy of Sheet C. Point out the headings from each label along the top of the grid. Show the children how to transfer the information from the report onto the grid (see below).

religion	leader	place of worship	beliefs	symbols	holy book	
Sikhism	Guru Nanak – first guru of ten	The gurdwara Langar – vegetarian meal served here	One god God is good God made the universe	Khanda The five Ks kesh kanga kara kachera kirpan	Guru Granth Sahib – the last guru	

Explain that you want them to use a grid like this to record their own information about a religion represented in their neighbourhood. Tell them that there is a blank column in case they think of additional information they would like to include. (The Sikhism grid could have a column about rules, for example.)

Divide the class into groups, perhaps friendship ones. Allocate a religion to each group from the list you made during the discussion. Give each group a blank grid (Sheet C) enlarged to A3. Remind them to write in note form.

Let the groups begin by brainstorming all that they can remember about their allocated religion. After ten minutes or so, provide the children with other ways of finding out about their religion; for example, looking in reference books, going to the library, using CD-Rom encyclopaedias, looking back at their own work completed in RE and so on. Anything they find out can be added to their grid.

Plenary

As a class, look at each group's grid. Ask members of the group to read out the key facts of information they have found out. Encourage the other groups to:

highlight the good points;

ask questions about the religion to clarify meaning;

add any extra information they might know;

add to or amend their planning grid with new ideas.

Tell the children that they will spend the next lesson using their grids to help them plan and write a group draft of their report on their religion.

Revving up

Learning objectives

■ To write a draft report as a group.

■ To write an introduction.

Resources

■ Sheet B (pages 42 and 43)

■ An enlarged recording grid from 'Switching on'

What to do

Display the enlarged copy of the grid on Sikhism from the 'Switching on' lesson and an enlarged version of Sheet B.

Begin the lesson by telling the children you are going to show them how to write a report using the recording grid and the text on Sikhism. Remind them that they will be writing and presenting their own finished reports as a group later.

Remember when doing shared writing to model gathering your ideas, rehearsing the sentence and reading it back, as well as paying attention to vocabulary choice.

The following is a script for your eyes only which you can use or adapt. The text in italics is what you say out loud as if to yourself; the text in bold is what you write.

I need a title that indicates to the reader what the report is going to be about. I could choose something simple, like 'Sikhism', or 'The Religion of Sikhism'. I think I am going to write this – **Finding out about Sikhism**.

We will be writing our introductions later so I am going to concentrate on the next paragraphs after the introduction. I am going to start by looking at my grid and giving myself the job of writing about the Sikhs' place of worship.

I am going to start by using the special word Sikhs have for their place of worship and defining it for my reader. **Sikhs meet to worship at a special place called a gurdwara. 'Gurdwara' means 'the door of the guru'.** *I think I need to say what the guru in the meeting place is. I'll write* **The guru in the place of worship is the Guru Granth Sahib; that is the holy book of the Sikhs.**

What verb tense am I writing in? That's right – the present tense. Now, I want to explain what happens in a gurdwara.'

The gurdwara serves as a place of worship, a school, a meeting room, a communal kitchen and, if necessary, a place for people to sleep.

Continue in this way until you have written two paragraphs. Explain that you now want them to write their own paragraphs in the same way about their religion. Tell them to go back to their groups and to each choose a different heading from the planning grid (they could work in pairs) and write the sentences for a paragraph about it. Explain that they also need to think about any diagrams and pictures they think would be useful in their report. Remind them that they will be writing the introduction and conclusion to their report as a group later on.

As they are writing, circulate around the groups, making sure they understand the task and how to use the grid to help them write their sentences. Ensure that in each group the children are working in pairs, each writing different paragraphs of the report. It would be helpful occasionally to read out some good examples of sentences to the others in order to share good work.

Plenary

Tell the children that they are going to finish this lesson by collectively writing the introduction to their report. Explain that you will demonstrate writing an introduction first and then it will be their turn.

Below is an example of a script you may use or amend:

The title of my report was 'Finding out about Sikhism'. Now I need a short paragraph to introduce the reader to Sikhism. An introduction is like a doorway and it sets the scene before a report goes into detail. It should give us information about 'who', 'what', 'where' and 'when'. I want to say what Sikhism actually is, where it began and what it is like today. What about … **The religion of Sikhism began in India over 500 years ago. It is now practised all over the world by Sikhs, followers of Sikhism**?

I'll just read that back. I think I need to add who started the religion, so I will insert the sentence, **Guru Nanak was the first spiritual leader.** *Now let's read that back.*

The religion of Sikhism began in India over 500 years ago. Guru Nanak was the first spiritual leader. It is now practised all over the world by Sikhs, followers of Sikhism. *Excellent. Now it is your turn!*

Explain to the children that you want them to write a few introductory sentences to their report as a group. Give them five minutes to agree the sentences and write their introductions.

Then, group by group, ask for a volunteer to read out the introductions. Ask the other groups to make positive comments and suggestions about how the introduction could be improved. The main consideration is whether the introduction tells the reader 'who', 'what', 'where', and 'when' information. Are the main terms to be used in the report defined?

Check through all the first drafts of the children's reports before the next lesson. It is a good idea for each group to have a folder labelled with the religion they are writing about, in which to keep all their pieces of text, diagrams and recording grids.

Taking off

Learning objective

■ To identify and use organisational devices in report writing.

Resources

■ Sheet A (pages 40 and 41)

■ Sticky notes

■ A3 paper, felt-tipped pens, scissors, glue

What to do

Start the lesson by reminding the children that, so far, they have gathered information about the different religions represented in the local area and mapped it out on a recording grid, used the grid to plan and write a draft copy of their report text and collectively written the introduction to their reports.

Ask for a volunteer from each group to read out their introduction in order to set the scene for the children.

Explain that today they are going to look at the different ways of organising information in a report. Ask them to look at an enlarged version of Sheet A with sticky notes covering the annotations. What different ways of organising information can they see in the text?

Remove the sticky note from each device on the text and discuss the purpose of each one: headings, subheadings, diagrams, labels, text boxes, bullet points and bold print.

Tell the children that for their independent work they are going to organise the text they have already written into a report format using some of the devices they have just identified.

Ask them to work in their groups as in previous lessons and to cut out their separate paragraphs that they have written. They then need to arrange the text on the A3 paper. Using the felt-tipped pens, they can add the organisational devices, such as subheadings, bullet points and text boxes. They might need to write notes on the paper to remind themselves that they want to use bullet points, or to put certain parts of the text in text boxes.

Once they are happy with the format they can glue everything into place. Each group needs to be prepared to show their draft report format to the other groups in the plenary and explain why they have used different organisational devices.

Circulate around the groups as they are doing this to ensure they are on task and to answer any questions they may have about the layout of the text.

Plenary

Ask each group to present their report format. Encourage different members of the groups to explain why they used a subheading here, or a text box there and so on.

Presenting their ideas in this way gives the children practice before they present their finished report to another class or in assembly.

Encourage the rest of the class to say what they like about the report format and how they think it could be improved. Questions to consider might be:

'Is the information presented clearly?'

'Would another diagram or picture be useful?'

'Does the diagram or picture need to be labelled?'

Finish the lesson by telling the class that in the next lesson they will be proofreading their report and then writing up their final copy.

Flying solo

Learning objectives

■ To identify the structural and linguistic features of a report.

■ To write a conclusion.

■ To proofread their own reports.

■ To write a final version of their report.

Resources

■ Sheet A (pages 40 and 41)

■ A3 draft copies of reports from 'Taking off'

■ Sticky notes

What to do

Tell the children that in today's lesson they will be finishing their reports and presenting them to the rest of the class in the plenary session. Explain that in order to do this they need to spend some time writing the conclusion and proofreading their reports before writing a final version.

Tell them that they are now going to collectively write the conclusion to their group report. Explain that you will demonstrate writing a conclusion first. Below is an example of a script you could use or amend. Again, the text in italics is what you say out loud as if to yourself; the text in bold is what you write.

All reports need a conclusion. A conclusion brings the report to an end and briefly summarises what has been said in the report. What about if I write… **The Sikh religion today has a following of over 20 million people and is ranked as the world's fifth largest religion?** *I'll just reread that to make sure it makes sense. I think I need to say where all the followers of Sikhism live. They live*

all over the world, so I'll add the word 'worldwide'. **The Sikh religion today has a following of over 20 million people worldwide and is ranked as the world's fifth largest religion.**

Brilliant! Now what else could we say for our conclusion?

Take suggestions from the children and then send the groups off to write their conclusion collaboratively. Give them five to ten minutes to complete the task and then move on to proofreading their reports. Explain that to help them proofread their work, you are going to look at some more features of report texts to make sure they include them in their own reports.

Display an enlarged version of Sheet A with the annotations covered with sticky notes. Discuss the structural features (introduction, non-chronological organisation, paragraphs organised according to categories of information and conclusion).

Next, give the children a few minutes to identify the special linguistic features of the report; they can talk to the children sitting near them and share their ideas. Take a number of answers and uncover the linguistic features as the children identify them (present tense, use of general nouns and pronouns, third person and factual writing with technical terms).

Next, explain that for their independent work they are going to proofread their piece of text using the checklist they have just discussed. Allow them time to work in their groups to do this, sharing their ideas.

Plenary

Ask the groups to take it in turns to present their finished reports to the rest of the class. Ask:

'What did you find easy about writing this report?'

'What did you find difficult?'

'What would you do differently if you had to write a report again?'

Give the children time in another lesson to write up their reports and prepare their presentation to another class or an assembly. They could use a word processor to produce their finished report.

Sheet A

title to say what the report is about

Sikhism

introduction to orientate the reader

Sikhism is a religion that was founded in a part of India called the Punjab in the early fifteenth century by a teacher called Guru Nanak. Today there are more than 20 million Sikhs worldwide. Sikh men are easily identified by their beards and turbans, which are an outward sign of their religious identity.

illustration to enhance meaning

general nouns and pronouns

third person

Sikhs follow the teachings of gurus. 'Guru' means 'spiritual leader'. Sikhs believe that there were ten special gurus, who came to the world to give God's teachings to man: Sikhs believe that these teachings show them the way to live. **Guru Nanak**, the first guru of the Sikhs, spent 20 years of his life travelling. Everywhere he went, he taught people that what matters is the way a person lives. Guru Nanak believed that all people were born equal and should have equal opportunities. He guided his people in the way of God's will, believing there was only one god.

information organised in paragraphs

The tenth guru said that there would be no more living gurus. Instead of a guru there would be the Sikhs' holy book, which is called **Guru Granth Sahib**. The holy book has the status of a guru and Sikhs show it the respect and devotion they would give to a human guru. It embodies the philosophy and fundamentals of Sikhism.

present tense

Sikhs believe:

words in bold to stand out

- in one god who is almighty and eternal;

- that God made the universe and everything in it;

bullet points to organise text

- that God is good, caring and present everywhere;

- that God is a spirit who should be loved and worshipped.

Sikhs have a few important rules:

- not to cut their hair;

- not to eat meat killed in the Muslim style;

- not to smoke, drink alcohol or take drugs other than those prescribed by a doctor as medicine.

Sheet A continued

Guru Gobind Singh, the last of the ten gurus, told all members of the Sikh brotherhood to wear the five Ks as a symbol to all of their faith.

(subheading)

Sikh symbol

The Sikh symbol is called a **khanda**. Two swords on the outside show that Sikhs should fight for what is right. Between them is a circle, which shows that God is one, and has no beginning or end. In the centre is a two-edged sword, also called a khanda, showing the power of God.

(labelled diagram)

The khanda

The Five Ks

Kesh means uncut hair. Sikhs let their hair grow as a symbol of their faith. During their lifetime it will get very long, so they wear a turban to keep it tidy.

The **kanga** is a small wooden comb used to keep their long hair tidy, and is a symbol of cleanliness. Combing their hair reminds Sikhs that their lives should be tidy and organised.

The **kara** is a steel bangle worn on the right arm. It is a closed circle with no beginning and no end, as with God there is no beginning and no end. The steel reminds them of the strength they must have when fighting for what is right.

Kachera are short trousers worn as underwear. The guru said they were a symbol that Sikhs were leaving old ideas behind and following new ones.

The **kirpan** is a short sword. It reminds Sikhs that they must fight against evil.

(text box)

(non-chronological organisation)

(factual writing using technical terms)

The **gurdwara** is a Sikh meeting place. 'Gurdwara' means 'the door of the guru'; the guru in the meeting place is the Guru Granth Sahib. The gurdwara serves as a place of worship, school, meeting room, communal kitchen and, if necessary, a place for people to sleep. The kitchen is a place where festival food, donated, prepared and cooked by the Sikh families of the community is shared with any visitors to the gurdwara on that day. This meal is always vegetarian and is called the **langar**.

(conclusion to sum up text)

The Sikh religion today has a following of over 20 million people worldwide and is ranked as the world's fifth largest religion. Sikhism preaches a message of devotion and remembrance of God at all times, truthful living and the equality of mankind. The religion is open to anyone through the holy book, the Guru Granth Sahib.

Sikhism

Sikhism is a religion that was founded in a part of India called the Punjab in the early fifteenth century by a teacher called Guru Nanak. Today there are more than 20 million Sikhs worldwide. Sikh men are easily identified by their beards and turbans, which are an outward sign of their religious identity.

Sikhs follow the teachings of gurus. 'Guru' means 'spiritual leader'. Sikhs believe that there were ten special gurus, who came to the world to give God's teachings to man: Sikhs believe that these teachings show them the way to live. **Guru Nanak**, the first guru of the Sikhs, spent 20 years of his life travelling. Everywhere he went, he taught people that what matters is the way a person lives. Guru Nanak believed that all people were born equal and should have equal opportunities. He guided his people in the way of God's will, believing there was only one god.

The tenth guru said that there would be no more living gurus. Instead of a guru there would be the Sikhs' holy book, which is called **Guru Granth Sahib**. The holy book has the status of a guru and Sikhs show it the respect and devotion they would give to a human guru. It embodies the philosophy and fundamentals of Sikhism.

Sikhs believe:

• in one god who is almighty and eternal;

• that God made the universe and everything in it;

• that God is good, caring and present everywhere;

• that God is a spirit who should be loved and worshipped.

Sikhs have a few important rules:

• not to cut their hair;

• not to eat meat killed in the Muslim style;

• not to smoke, drink alcohol or take drugs other than those prescribed by a doctor as medicine.

Guru Gobind Singh, the last of the ten gurus, told all members of the Sikh brotherhood to wear the five Ks as a symbol to all of their faith.

Sikh symbol

The Sikh symbol is called a **khanda**. Two swords on the outside show that Sikhs should fight for what is right. Between them is a circle, which shows that God is one, and has no beginning or end. In the centre is a two edged sword, also called a khanda, showing the power of God.

The khanda

The Five Ks

Kesh means uncut hair. Sikhs let their hair grow as a symbol of their faith. During their lifetime it will get very long, so they wear a turban to keep it tidy.

The **kanga** is a small wooden comb used to keep their long hair tidy, and is a symbol of cleanliness. Combing their hair reminds Sikhs that their lives should be tidy and organised.

The **kara** is a steel bangle worn on the right arm. It is a closed circle with no beginning and no end, as with God there is no beginning and no end. The steel reminds them of the strength they must have when fighting for what is right.

Kachera are short trousers worn as underwear. The guru said they were a symbol that Sikhs were leaving old ideas behind and following new ones.

The **kirpan** is a short sword. It reminds Sikhs that they must fight against evil.

The **gurdwara** is a Sikh meeting place. 'Gurdwara' means 'the door of the guru'; the guru in the meeting place is the Guru Granth Sahib. The gurdwara serves as a place of worship, school, meeting room, communal kitchen and, if necessary, a place for people to sleep. The kitchen is a place where festival food, donated, prepared and cooked by the Sikh families of the community is shared with any visitors to the gurdwara on that day. This meal is always vegetarian and is called the **langar**.

The Sikh religion today has a following of over 20 million people worldwide and is ranked as the world's fifth largest religion. Sikhism preaches a message of devotion and remembrance of God at all times, truthful living and the equality of mankind. The religion is open to anyone through the holy book, the Guru Granth Sahib.

Sheet C

	religion
	leader
	place of worship
	beliefs
	symbols
	holy book

Chapter 3

Instruction writing

What is an instruction text?

Instructions tell someone how to do or make something. The success of the instructions can be judged by how easily the reader (or listener) can follow the procedure successfully.

Structural features

- Heading and subheadings
- List of items required
- Sequence of steps to be carried out in order
- Often has labelled diagrams

Linguistic features

- Usually in the present tense
- Sentences begin with an imperative verb, 'you' or a time connective such as 'then', 'next' or 'after that'
- Clear and concise - no unnecessary adjectives, adverbs or 'flowery' language
- In time order

Examples of instruction texts

- recipes
- technical manuals (such as for a television)
- instructions for games
- directions
- sewing or knitting patterns

Teaching instruction writing

One of the fundamental challenges of teaching children to write instructions is to help them consider purpose, audience and form. It is essential that they consider the prior knowledge and needs of their intended readers in order to write effective instructions that the readers can follow. Stress the importance of thinking yourself into the mind of the reader and anticipating their needs. A bit like with poetry, children need to exercise some discipline in choosing just the right words and exercising economy of words so that their sentences are generally simple with clear sequencing and precise language that can be easily understood by the reader. It is good to have readers using the instructions to test out the extent of the success of the writing.

While it is generally taught that instructions begin with an imperative verb, they can also begin with the word 'you' or a time connective, such as 'next'. Children should be given freedom to judge which sort of sentence beginning is most appropriate. There is a good opportunity here to discuss the differences between the two different forms of instructional communications – speaking and listening and writing and reading – and the demands they make upon children.

Instruction writing – progression

Simple instructions are introduced in Key Stage 1. (Reception: T15; Year 1, Term 1: T13, T16; Year 2, Term 1: T13, T14, T15, T16, T17, T18).

In Year 3 children evaluate different types of instructional texts and are introduced to a range of organisational devices when writing instructions, such as lists, bullet points and keys (Term 2: T12, T13, T14, T15, T16).

In **Year 4** the key features of instructional texts are taught (Term 1: T22) and children learn to write instructions using linking phrases and organisational devices, such as subheadings and numbers (Term 1: T25, T26).

In Year 5 (Term 1: T22, T25) and Year 6 (Term 3: T19, T22) children are moving on to writing and testing instructions, by revising the structure, organisational and presentational devices and language features of their instructions.

Unit 1

Lesson focus

Design and Technology Unit 4b – Storybooks

Overall aim

To analyse the main features of instruction texts and to write instructions to make a storybook.

Design and Technology emphasis

In this unit the children will learn to build and assemble a range of simple mechanisms, such as levers and linkages, in order to make a book with moving parts. They will develop their ability to work in groups, listening and respecting others' ideas, as they decide what type of book they are making and share out the tasks.

Literacy links

Year 4, Term 1: T22, T25, T26, S2, S4

About this unit

In this unit the writing of instructions is explored in a practical context – by making a storybook the children have first-hand experience of the task they are describing. Features of instruction writing that are highlighted include the use of the imperative verb and organisational devices.

This unit builds on D&T Units 1A 'Moving pictures' and Unit 3A 'Packaging'. The children need to have experience of hinges and sliders, and to be able to use basic cutting tools to join and cut paper and card, before making their storybook.

The lessons should be undertaken after the design and make assignment of the storybook unit.

Switching on

Learning objective

- To identify the key structural and linguistic features of an instruction text.

Resources

- Sheets A, B and C (pages 51 to 53)
- Coloured pencils and highlighters
- A collection of instructions from different sources, such as recipes, for assembling something and for playing games
- A collection of books or greetings cards with pop-ups and moving parts

What to do

Begin by recalling with the children the work they are doing in design and technology on designing and making a storybook with moving parts. Explain that over the next few lessons they are going to find out more about how to write instructions and then write their own instructions to make a storybook with a moving part.

Ask them if they have read books with moving parts before. What are their favourites? What do they enjoy about them? Take two or three responses and then show them the collection of greetings cards and books with pop-ups and moving parts. Briefly discuss the different designs, asking questions such as 'Which parts are moving?', 'How do you think it is made?' and 'How are the moving parts joined together?'

Display an enlarged copy of Sheet B. Before reading the text, ask the children to tell you if they know immediately what type of text it is. How do they know?

Involve the class in reading the text. As you read, stop to check the children's understanding of the text and individual word definitions. If there are words they do not understand the meaning of, demonstrate using a dictionary to find the definition.

Discuss the text in general. Do the children think the instructions are clear? Are the diagrams useful? Do they think they could successfully make the card following these directions?

Explain that they will have an opportunity to try them out soon but first they are going to look more closely at the text to find out about the special writing features of instructional texts.

Ask several children to reread sections of the text aloud. Using Sheet A (the annotated version) as a prompt for your eyes only, pick out the structural and linguistic features of the instructions. Annotate the enlarged copy (using one coloured pen for the structural features and another for the linguistic features). Make sure the children understand each feature by sharing samples of other instructions from the collection.

Provide pairs of children with copies of different types of instructional texts from the collection and then ask: 'Can you find the headings and subheadings?', 'What imperative verbs can you see in the texts?', 'How long are the sentences?', 'What organisational features are used?' (for example, numbering) and 'Do they use diagrams?'

Now, display an enlarged copy of the 'Instructions quiz' (Sheet C). Explain that the page has a collection of extracts on it – all from different instructional texts. Tell the children that you want them to work in pairs (mixed ability) to complete the following tasks. It is useful to have the tasks written up on the board.

1. Read all the instruction extracts; check any tricky word definitions in a dictionary;

2. Match the instructions to the correct pictures;

3. Write down the purpose of each extract. For example, 'To give directions';

4. Underline all the imperative verbs;

5. Highlight examples of time connectives.

Give each pair their own copy of Sheet C to do the tasks. Early finishers can write down further examples of time connectives using a thesaurus or from finding them in the collection of instruction leaflets or books.

Work with a group of children requiring support and complete the task as a group.

Plenary

Begin by discussing the purpose of each instruction extract. Then ask the children how many imperative verbs they found. Take five or six examples to underline on the enlarged copy of the quiz. How many time connectives

did they highlight? Again, take a number of examples and highlight them on the enlarged copy of the quiz.

Finish by making a list of time connectives; this will be useful when the children are writing their own instructions.

In a design and technology lesson, ask the children to follow the instructions to make the pop-up card.

Revving up

Learning objectives

■ To identify verbs and adverbs. To use adverbs in instructions.

■ To improve some instructions.

■ To follow instructions.

Resources

■ Sheets C to E (pages 53 to 55)

■ The pull lever card already made from following the instructions on Sheet E

What to do

Before the lesson, make the pull lever card from Sheet E yourself to use as a demonstration.

Remind the children about the instruction quiz they did in the previous lesson. Display an enlarged copy of it (Sheet C). Ask them to point out all the verbs in the text. Explain that the action of the verb can be described more fully by using an adverb. Find some in the text, such as 'carefully melt' and 'gradually work'. Ask the children to find the others. Ask them how they help the instructions.

Next, display an enlarged version of Sheet D (page 54). Show the children the completed card with a pull lever (the one you made earlier). Tell them that the instructions on Sheet D describe how to make the card. Read out the three sets of instructions. Discuss with the children which example (1, 2 or 3) would be the best to use if they wanted to make the card themselves. Ask them to give their reasons why. Points to draw out are: the layout of the instructions – whether they are easy to follow, information about materials and measurements needed, how clear and concise the language is and whether there is irrelevant (or missing) information.

Disassemble the card and show the children how you made it, briefly talking through each step. Then, explain that they are going to work in pairs using a copy of the instructions in Example 2. Tell them that you want them to improve the instructions by adding appropriate adverbs and labelling the diagrams. You might want the children to use a thesaurus in order to get a wide range of different adverbs.

Set them off on the right track by reading the first instruction and asking them to think of an appropriate adverb to add. Take a few examples and select one to insert. Look at the first diagram and discuss what it shows and what needs labelling. Label it clearly and concisely; for example, indicating the measurements of each slot.

Send the children away to complete the task in pairs. As you move around the class, highlight good examples of adverbs and check that the diagram labelling is not too detailed.

Plenary

Ask for volunteers to read out their instructions and discuss briefly why these are better than the originals. Highlight the use of time connectives, adverbs and adjectives to clarify meaning.

Give the children time to make the card following their improved instructions.

Taking off

Learning objective

■ To begin writing own instructions.

Resources

■ Sheets A, B and F (pages 51, 52 and 56)

■ The children's own storybooks with moveable parts

What to do

Before this lesson, the children need to have completed making their storybooks with moveable parts in their design and technology lessons.

Tell them that they are going to use what they have found out about instructions to write their own instructions for making their storybook. Explain that the purpose of this is so that someone else could make their storybook.

Explain that to help them get started you are going to begin writing the instructions together as a class. First, refer the children to the text they explored in 'Switching on' (Sheet B) to remind themselves of the structural and linguistic features of an instructional text. Share an enlarged version of this page and, using the teachers' annotated page (Sheet A) as your prompt, ask them to recall the structural and linguistic features of instruction texts. Highlight these features on the enlarged copy and leave up as a prompt for the children.

Next, begin to write the instructions. Explain that they could use a writing frame to help them. Show them an enlarged version of Sheet F.

Following is a script for your eyes only which you can use or adapt. The text in italics is what you say out loud as if to yourself, the text in bold is what you write.

Right, what is the first thing I need to do? That's right – decide on the title of my instructions.

Take suggestions from the children and complete the title; for example, 'How to make a book with moveable parts'. Then continue:

Now, I need to write the aim – that is what I am going to achieve. Well, my finished product is a storybook with moving parts…

Encourage the children to give you answers and select one; for example:

How to make a storybook that incorporates a pull lever.

Carry on to complete the list of materials required. Ask the children what they needed to make their storybooks. Write their responses horizontally across the line, until someone points out that they need to be in a vertical list so that it is easy for the reader to collect the materials and equipment. Make sure they remember that the materials need to be detailed; for example, the measurements or size of paper used to make the book.

The storybooks that the children have made may require detailed instructions so tell them that you want them to select just one moving part of the book and write the instructions for that. Briefly map out how they could break down the making of the moving part of their book into small steps and then provide them with ideas for beginning the writing. For example:

Take a piece of thin card and fold it in half. Press the fold down.

Ask *Can you think of a time connective to add to the sentence?* and *Is an adverb needed anywhere?* For example, **<u>First</u>, take a piece of thin card and <u>accurately</u> fold it in half. Press the fold down <u>firmly</u>.**

Answer any queries the children might have and send them off to start their work. Select a group to sit and work with. Prompt the children to include adverbs, time connectives and clear, concise language.

Plenary

Ask for volunteers to read out what they have written. Highlight the linguistic features and good practice. Encourage the class to help each other improve their work – different time connectives, additional adverbs, shorter sentences and so on.

Flying solo

Learning objective

■ To complete a set of instructions including diagrams and organisational devices.

Resources

■ Sheets B and F (pages 52 and 56)

What to do

Begin the lesson by telling the children that today they are going to finish their instructions. Give them a few minutes to read through the instructions they began in 'Taking off' to refresh their memories of what they have written.

Next, display an enlarged copy of a child's instructions – one that you have previously chosen as representative of the class containing all the points you want to draw out for revision. Alongside it display an enlarged copy of Sheet B (page 52). Point out the key features of instruction texts that the child has used; for example, adverbs and time connectives. Then suggest ways of improving the work.

Tell the class that they now need to finish writing their own instructions. Ask *'What else could you add to your instructions to complete them?'* (You want them to include diagrams and organisational devices.)

Ask the class to suggest some different organisational devices they could use – bullet points, numbered steps, subheadings and so on. Then, ask the child whose work you have displayed what they are going to use and demonstrate this on his or her instructions.

Then move on to discuss diagrams. Emphasise the point that diagrams need to be simple, clear and labelled. Point out that not all steps in the instructions need to be illustrated with a diagram but that it is a good idea to have a picture of the finished product. Illustrate the child's work on display with a diagram, if you wish.

Answer any queries the children might have and set them off on their task.

Select a different group from the one you worked with in 'Taking off' to sit with and support to enhance their work. It might be necessary to circulate around the class at intervals during the independent work to ensure that the children are on the right track to complete their instructions. Points to look out for are: too many and too detailed instructions and too small and too detailed diagrams.

Plenary

Display an instruction text with spelling errors in it. Ask the children to identify a word they think might not be spelled correctly. Ask for volunteers to write alternative suggestions on the board. Ask how the children can find out which is the correct spelling – ask someone, look at classroom displays and in dictionaries.

Ask the children to work in pairs to look at their instructions and each find one word where they are unsure of the spelling. Ask them to find the correct spelling.

Finish off the lesson by reflecting with the children upon what they have learned about writing instructional texts. Some of the areas for discussion could be: structure of the text, imperative verbs, adverbs, time connectives, organisational devices and the use of diagrams.

How to make a talking mouth pop-up card

title and aim – a statement of what is to be achieved

You will need

thin card (A4 size)
pencil
ruler
scissors
glue
paper
coloured pencils for decorations

quantities or dimensions stated explicitly

list of materials needed

What to do

sub-heading

1. Start by taking the thin piece of card and accurately fold it in half. Crease the fold down firmly.

2. Using a ruler, carefully measure halfway along the fold (Figure 1). Mark this point with a dot. Now, draw a line from the dot, about 2cm long, out towards the edge of the card, and cut along it.

adverb used to clarify meaning

Figure 1

3. Fold the two cut edges back in a triangle shape (Figure 2).

4. Next, open the card again. You will have two triangles with a cut in the middle.

numbers to indicate a sequence of steps to follow

imperative verb

5. Lastly, push the two folded edges of one triangle through, in towards the middle. Repeat this with the other triangle (Figure 3).

Figure 2

short, simple sentences

time connective

6. You will have something that looks like an open mouth, around which a person or animal can be drawn. The mouth could be the open beak of a bird or you could add a set of paper teeth and make it into a crocodile. You could make it into a pelican with a fish in its mouth or a fish with bubbles coming out of its mouth.

Figure 3

diagrams to aid understanding

illustration of final product to help reader understand what is to be achieved

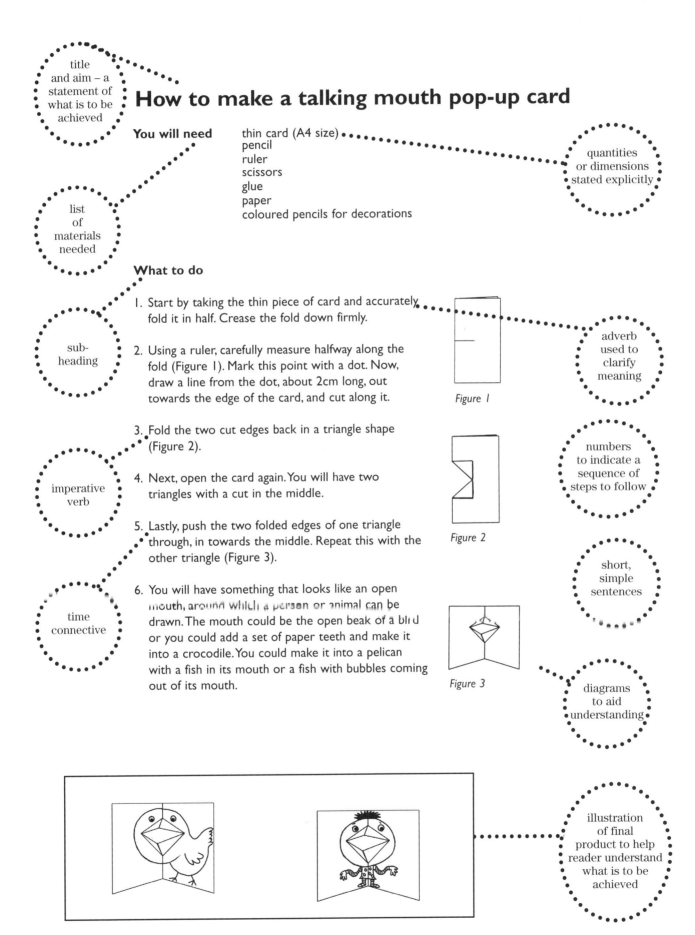

How to make a talking mouth pop-up card

You will need   thin card (A4 size)

pencil

ruler

scissors

glue

paper

coloured pencils for decorations

What to do

1. Start by taking the thin piece of card and accurately fold it in half. Crease the fold down firmly.

Figure 1

2. Using a ruler, carefully measure halfway along the fold (Figure 1). Mark this point with a dot. Now, draw a line from the dot, about 2cm long, out towards the edge of the card, and cut along it.

3. Fold the two cut edges back in a triangle shape (Figure 2).

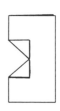

Figure 2

4. Next, open the card again. You will have two triangles with a cut in the middle.

5. Lastly, push the two folded edges of one triangle through, in towards the middle. Repeat this with the other triangle (Figure 3).

6. You will have something that looks like an open mouth, around which a person or animal can be drawn. The mouth could be the open beak of a bird or you could add a set of paper teeth and

Figure 3

make it into a crocodile. You could make it into a pelican with a fish in its mouth or a fish with bubbles coming out of its mouth.

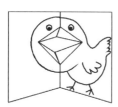

Instructions quiz

1. Carefully melt margarine over a low heat.

2. Next, gradually work in dry ingredients. Stir the mixture thoroughly.

3. Finally, press firmly into a greased cake tin.

---

9. Then, open the right flap. Bend its bottom point up accurately along the creases you have just made. Squash the paper flat.

10. Now repeat step 9 very neatly with the flap on the left.

11. Next, fold down the tip of the head. Then, reverse fold it inside the neck.

First, empty all the contents into a saucepan. Thoroughly scrape out the tin with a spatula.

Now, gently put the pan over a low heat.

Then, heat gently, stirring occasionally. DO NOT ALLOW TO BOIL.

After two minutes, carefully remove the pan from the heat and serve immediately.

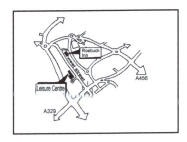

- After leaving the A329, turn left at the traffic lights along West Street.

- Slowly continue on past the Leisure Centre on the left until you come to the Roebuck Inn.

- Then, at the pub turn sharp right up a narrow lane.

Trace the sun design onto thick card and carefully cut out with a sharp knife and a metal ruler.

Draw neatly round the template on the paper and cut out the design.

Fold the shape between the points towards the centre, overlapping evenly.

Redialling a number

To quickly redial the phone number last called, firmly press the green telephone button twice.

Sheet D

Example 1

card

card, ruler, scissors

Carefully make two slits. Then, make a pull strip shaped like a flapping wing. Slot pull strip through the slits and firmly pull!

Example 2

Instructions to make a card with a pull lever

You will need   *2 pieces of thin card (A4)*

                    a pair of scissors

                    a ruler

                    a pencil

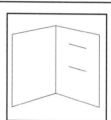

1. Fold one piece of card in half. Crease the fold.

2. On one side of the card make two cuts, 3cm long.

3. Using the other piece of card, make a pull strip 3cm wide.

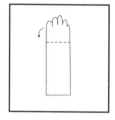

4. Cut out a wing shape at the top of the pull strip. Then fold the strip just
   below the wing and crease the fold.

5. Slot the pull strip through the cut slits.

6. Moving the pull strip makes the wing flap.

Example 3

How to make a card with a pull lever

You need to fold a thin piece of A4 card in half and press down the crease. The card can be any colour. Then you measure, using a ruler, two slits on one side of the card where you want your lever picture to be. The slits need to be the same width as the pull strip. They should not be too near the edge of the page or too close together as the pull lever will not work and will look silly.

Next, you make a pull lever by cutting a strip of card the same width as the two slits. It can be as long as you like. Draw a wing shape at the top of the pull lever and cut it out. Make a crease just below the wing. Insert the pull strip through the cut slits and move the pull strip up and down to make the wing flap.

Instructions to make a card with a pull lever

You will need: 2 pieces of thin card (A4)

a pair of scissors

a ruler

a pencil

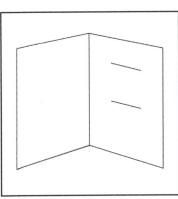

Figure 1

1. Fold one piece of card in half. Crease the fold.

2. On one side of the card make two cuts, 3cm long. (Figure 1)

3. Using the other piece of card, make a pull strip 3cm wide.

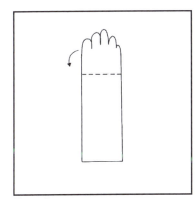

Figure 2

4. Cut out a wing shape at the top of the pull strip. Then fold the strip just below the wing and crease the fold. (Figure 2)

5. Slot the pull strip through the cut slits.

6. Moving the pull strip makes the wing flap. (Figure 3)

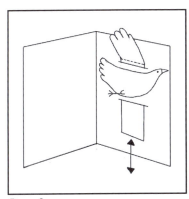

Figure 3

Sheet F

Title _____

Aim

You will need

Unit 2

Lesson focus

Physical Education Unit 11 – Invasion games

Overall aim

To analyse the main features of instruction texts and to devise a game involving throwing and catching. To write the instructions for the game so that other people can play it.

Physical Education emphasis

In this unit the children will learn simple attacking tactics and defensive movements using a range of equipment through playing competitive games. They will develop ball handling skills, strategies and tactics in order to outwit the opposition and score a goal!

Literacy links

Year 4, Term 1: T22, T25, T26, S2, S4

About this unit

This unit uses PE lessons to develop the content for writing instructions in literacy lessons. The children have to write the instructions for playing an invasion game they have previously developed in PE – thus providing them with a real purpose for writing.

The unit is divided into separate PE and literacy lessons that can be taught alongside each other over the period of a week.

Switching on

Learning objectives

■ To read and understand instructions for a game.

■ To play the game.

Resources

■ Sheet A (pages 61 and 62), cut out and mounted on card

■ Playground or large hall

■ Netballs or footballs

What to do

In a PE lesson:
Once the children have changed and have completed their warm-up session, remind them of the work they have been previously doing in PE lessons to develop their throwing and catching skills.

Explain that today they are going to put these throwing and catching skills into practice by playing some team games. Tell them that some of the team games are invasion games where teams enter their opponents' territory and try to get into good positions for shooting or reaching the 'goal'.

Explain that they are going to read and interpret instructions for a team game in their groups. Ask *'Have you read and used instructions for any other games?'*, *'How do you teach each other games in the playground?'* (oral instructions) and *'What special features are you expecting to see in the sets of instructions?'* (equipment, rules).

Tell the class that over the next few lessons in literacy and PE they will find out about the special features of instructions and that they are going to write their own instructions describing how to play a team game they have made up themselves.

Give out the instructions for the games on Sheet A, dividing the class into the required number per game as you go. Different groups can play the same game.

Tell each group to start by reading through the instructions carefully, then collect the equipment they require to play the game and finally learn how to play the game in order to demonstrate it to the rest of the class at the end of the lesson.

As you circulate around the groups your teaching points need to include:

Have they read and interpreted the instructions correctly?

Why is there a section on rules?

Have they thought of anything to add to the instructions? How to score?

What variations could be made to the game? Different equipment, different rules?

Finish the lesson with a cooling down session.

Plenary

Gather all the class together and ask each group in turn to read out their instructions and then demonstrate their game.

Ask for positive feedback from the rest of the groups about the group's interpretation of the instructions and their game. Points to make include:

'What skills was the game developing?'

'Were the instructions easy to understand? Why? Why not?'

'How do you know what equipment to use?'

'Why do you need rules?'

'Did you need to make up any more rules, such as how to score or penalties for breaking rules?'

'Can anyone think of any variations that could be made to the game – using different equipment, different sized balls, making up different rules?'

'How can you improve the game?' (Use different passes. Use different dodges. Limit the area played in.) *'How can you include this in the instructions for the games? Coaching tips?'*

Revving Up

Learning objective

■ To identify the structural and linguistic features of instructions.

Resources

■ 2 or 3 copies of Sheet B (page 63), cut up into cards

■ A collection of instructions for games

■ A3 paper, felt-tipped pens

What to do

In a literacy lesson:
Begin by recalling with the children the team games they played in their PE lesson. Explain that now they are going to find out more about how to write instructions and then make up their own team game and write the instructions for it.

Ask them to tell their partners two or three things that they already know about the genre of instructions. Then ask a few children to tell the class what they already knew and what they have learned from their partner.

Next, brainstorm other types of instructions (recipes, directions and so on) used in daily life. Write these on the board.

Then, ask the children to tell you how they would expect instructions to be written and organised. Accept a couple of suggestions (such as title, numbered or bulleted points, list of materials/resources, and time connectives). Write these on the board.

Ask the children to get into their PE groups. Provide each group with some sets of instructions from the collection and ask them to make a list of any of these special features of instructions they find, giving examples.

After ten minutes, give each group two or three instructions features cards from Sheet B. Ask someone from each group to read out a feature and discuss its meaning as a class. Make sure they understand what each feature card means. You may like to use an enlarged copy of one of the instructions from the collection to demonstrate each feature.

Next, ask the children to find examples of these features in their sets of instructions. For example, for the feature card 'time connectives' they might find the words 'then', 'next' and 'finally' in their instructions.

Plenary

Ask the groups of children to call out the structural features of instructions they have identified first and then the linguistic features. List them on the board. Remind the children of the purpose of each feature. For example, ask *'What is the purpose of the title?'* (a statement of what is to be achieved) and *'What verb form is used?'* (the imperative).

Next, take each feature in turn and ask different groups to give an example from their set of instructions of that feature.

Finish by telling the children that in the next two lessons they will be devising their own team game and rules. Then they will write out the instructions for their game for the other groups to play, using the special features of instructional writing they have identified today.

Taking off

Learning objectives

■ To make up a team game in PE.

■ To write the instructions for the game.

Resources

■ Sheet B (page 63), not cut up into cards

■ Playground or large hall

■ Variety of PE equipment, such as balls, hoops, beanbags

■ A3 paper, felt-tipped pens

What to do

In a PE lesson:

Tell the children that they are now going to make up their own team game and write the instructions for that game. Explain that the purpose of this is so that other groups can read their instructions and play the game. Encourage the children to keep the game simple – perhaps a variation of the game they played in 'Switching on', using different rules or different equipment.

Show the children the equipment available to choose from. Explain any special parameters you want them to consider, such as size of space allocated to play the game. Brainstorm a few ideas for games with the class to get them started. Then, give the groups five minutes to sit and discuss their ideas. Encourage them to start testing out their ideas and playing the game. Circulate round the groups. Some may need extra help to get them started – give them an outline of a game.

Tell the children that once they have played their game several times they should show it to you. After you have seen it and commented, ask them to begin writing down the instructions to play the game on a large sheet of paper. Suggest that each team member takes a turn to write a different section of the instructions with all members contributing to the ideas, spelling, punctuation and layout. This may take a couple of PE lessons or need to be finished in a literacy lesson.

Plenary

Ask all the groups to stick up their instructions on a wall. Give them time to circulate and look at each other's examples of instructions. Tell them that they are looking for the special features of instruction writing in each other's examples – have they included them all? (Display an enlarged version of Sheet B for them to refer to.)

Then, give the groups time to add to or change their own instructions. You need to make sure the groups' instructions are well presented before the next lesson because other children will have to read and follow them.

Flying Solo

Learning objectives

- To play the PE games using the sets of instructions written by the children.
- To evaluate the instructions.

Resources

- Sheet B (page 63), not cut up into cards
- The sets of instructions written by the children
- Playground or large hall
- Equipment needed for the games

What to do

In a PE lesson:
Tell the children that today in their groups they are going to play each other's team games.

Give out the instructions, making sure the game can be played by the number of people in that group.

Tell them to start by reading through the instructions, collect the equipment they require and then learn to play the game.

Once they have played the game several times ask each group to sit down, have a rest and look at the instructions. Ask them to consider the following questions:

> 'What was good about the instructions?'
>
> 'What could have made the instructions better?'
>
> 'Were there any rules included?'
>
> 'Were the instructions easy to follow?'
>
> 'Was anything important left out?'

(These questions could be written up for the children to refer to.) Tell them to think about the special features of instructional writing as they discuss these points.

Plenary

Ask each group to read out their new sets of instructions and demonstrate the team game. Ask each group to make a positive point about the instructions and also suggest a way they could have been improved.

Finish the lesson with a cooling down session. After the children have changed, reflect upon what they have learned during their work about how instructions are constructed.

Some of the areas for discussion could be: how instructions are organised, linguistic features of instructions and how different kinds of instructions vary in format.

Sheet A

Game 1   2 v 2

The aim is for two players to pass the ball to each other, while moving about. The other two players, the opponents, are trying to intercept the ball.

Equipment: one large ball

                 four players

- Decide on teams of two.
- Player 1 starts off with the ball.
- Then, Player 2 on his or her team quickly runs into a space.
- Player 1 throws Player 2 the ball.
- Meanwhile, Players 3 and 4, the opponents, try to catch the ball by intercepting it, before Player 2 catches it.

Rules: No contact. No running with the ball.

Game 2   2 v 1

The aim is for two players to pass the ball to each other, while moving about. The other player, the opponent, is trying to intercept the ball.

Equipment: one large ball

             three players

- Decide on the first team of two players.
- Player 1 starts off with the ball.
- Then, Player 2 on his team quickly runs into a space.
- Player 1 throws Player 2 the ball.
- Meanwhile, Player 3, the opponent, tries to catch the ball by intercepting it, before Player 2 catches it. If Player 3 is successful, Player 2 then becomes the opponent who is trying to intercept the ball.

Rules: No contact. No running with the ball.

Game 3   Bull's-eye!

The aim is for each team to score points by throwing a ball using a chest pass at a target on a wall. Each team member has five throws. The opposing team keeps score for the team playing.

Equipment: one large ball

teams of two players (four players in all)

a wall, different coloured chalk, metre rule

1. Decide on teams of two.
2. Accurately draw a 1 metre diameter circle on a wall. In the middle of the circle draw and fill in a large bull's-eye.
3. Then, mark a line about 3 metres away from the circle from behind which to throw the ball.
4. Team 1 takes it in turns to throw the ball five times each at the target using a chest pass.
5. Meanwhile, Team 2 keeps score.

Rules: 5 points for a bull's-eye, 2 points if the ball hits inside the circle, bonus point if the ball is caught as it rebounds. Shoulder or chest passes only.

Game 4   Beat the ball!

The aim is for a child to run round the outside of the circle while a ball is being passed inside the circle, and to try and beat the ball.

Equipment: one large ball

six players

1. Stand in a circle with one player holding the ball in the middle of the circle.
2. Another player is chosen to stand on the outside of the circle behind another child.
3. This player must run round the outside of the circle while the ball is passed from the centre to each child, who throws it back to the centre each time.
4. The ball needs to be passed carefully in the same direction as the player runs: he or she must try to beat the ball.
5. If the ball is dropped, the runner is the winner. If the runner beats the ball back to the start position, then the runner also wins.
6. A new runner and thrower are chosen and takes their positions to start again.

title or aims	anonymous reader

a list of things needed	present tense

sentences that begin with:

- imperative verb (for example, 'cut', 'put', 'make')
- 'you'
- a time connective (for example, 'first', 'next', 'finally')

sequence of steps of what to do in time order

bullet points or numbering

short, simple sentences	subheadings

clear, concise language	diagram

Explanation writing

What is an explanation text?

An explanation tells us how something happens or why something happens.

Structural features

- Title to tell the reader what the text will be about
- Usually has an opening statement to set the scene
- A series of logical steps explaining the process
- Often has diagrams

Linguistic features

- Usually present tense (except in historical explanations)
- Third person (impersonal) style
- Often uses the passive
- Uses causal connectives (such as 'because', 'in order to', 'as a result of', 'consequently', 'which means that') to show cause and effect
- Use of time or sequential connectives to aid chronological order ('firstly', 'afterwards', 'meanwhile', 'subsequently', 'finally')
- Technical vocabulary
- Complex sentences

Examples of explanation texts

- write-ups of science experiments
- encyclopaedia entries
- technical manuals
- textbooks
- non-fiction books

Teaching explanation writing

When children write explanations they have two main hurdles to leap. First, they have to be able to grasp the concept they are trying to explain, which requires some complex thinking skills, and then they have to articulate their understanding in the fairly rigid conventions of the written explanation genre. Plenty of opportunities to speak their explanation before writing will help them to organise their thoughts. Sharing their explanation with response partners at different stages during the writing process will give them a live audience to help them identify 'gaps' in their explanation and reveal specialised vocabulary that has not been clearly defined.

Making flow charts or simple diagrams helps to develop the children's own understanding of the process they are explaining as well as helping the reader understand the text more easily.

Explanation writing – progression

Children are introduced to explanations in Year 2 (Term 2: T17, T19, T20, T21) where they are required to read and make simple flow charts or diagrams that explain a process.

In Year 3 children develop their note taking skills (Term 1: T20, T21; Term 2: T17) into making simple records, including flow charts.

In **Year 4** children are introduced to the key structural and linguistic features of a range of explanation texts (Term 2: T20). They are also encouraged to improve the cohesion of their written explanations through the use of paragraphing, link phrases and organisational devices such as subheadings and numbering (Term 2: T24, T25).

In Year 5 children are required to read a range of explanatory texts, noting features of the genre (Term 2: T15), as well as planning and writing their own explanation texts (Term 2: T22).

In Year 6 children read and write explanation texts, focusing on the use of impersonal formal language (Term 3: T15, T16).

Unit 1

Lesson focus

Science Unit 4d – Solids and liquids and how they can be separated

Overall aim

To identify the features of an explanation text and to write an explanation about the processes of freezing and melting.

Science emphasis

In this unit the children learn about the characteristics of solids and liquids. They learn about the process of filtering by discovering how a tea bag works. They investigate the processes of freezing and melting. They use scientific ideas and vocabulary to explain everyday experiences and they develop recording skills through the use of mind maps.

Literacy links

Year 4, Term 2: T19, T20, T24, T25, S4

About this unit

In this unit the children are asked to explain the processes of freezing and melting. They are taught to draw diagrams to illustrate their answers. The lessons focus on the key features of an explanation text – purpose, structure, language and presentation.

The science emphasis of the unit builds on work completed in Unit 3C 'Characteristics of materials' and links to Unit 4C 'Keeping warm'. It is helpful if children are used to describing materials and are familiar with the processes of melting and freezing.

Switching on

Learning objectives

■ To read, enjoy and understand an explanation text.

■ To identify the key structural features of an explanation text.

■ To draw up guidelines on how to write an explanation.

Resources

■ Sheets A to C (pages 71 to 73)

■ A collection of explanation texts from a variety of sources

What to do

Begin by reminding the children of the work they have been doing in science on solids and liquids. Then move on to explain that over the next few lessons they will find out about the special features of explanation texts, before writing their own, answering the question 'How can you turn water into ice?'

Next, tell the children that you have an example of an explanation text for them to look at. Display just the title of an enlarged version of Sheet B and say 'I want you to read the title of this explanation text and predict what you

think the text will be about and what it might say.' Listen to a few suggestions and then tell them they will now find out if they are right.

Read the shared text aloud. As you read, stop after a couple of paragraphs to check the children's understanding of the content of the text through questioning. For example, stop after the first two paragraphs and ask 'What do you think the phrase "specific seasonal variations in temperature" means?' Explain anything the children do not understand.

Make sure the children understand all the vocabulary used in the text. Underline some words and model looking them up in a dictionary, clarifying the meaning of any difficult ones. For example, ask 'What does "acid soils" mean?' Listen to a suggestion and then say, 'Let's see if you are right by looking it up in the dictionary.' Model this and read out the definition to the children, checking that they understand it in the context of the text.

Ask the children, 'Why has the author used scientific words and phrases in the text?' (Authors use technical vocabulary in explanations in order to explain processes accurately.)

When you have finished reading the text, ask 'What other kinds of explanation texts can you think of?' Together with the children, brainstorm other examples of explanation texts and make a list. For example, textbooks, technical manuals and encyclopaedias.

Explain that now you are going to look more closely at the text to find out about some of the special features that make it an explanation text.

Begin by reading the title and asking the children what is special about it. (It is a question.) Tell them that titles of explanation texts often ask a question or define the process they are going to explain. Show them a few examples of titles from the selection of explanation texts you have collected for the lesson.

Continue through the text in this way, highlighting the structural features as shown on Sheet A and listed below:

- a title which asks a question or sometimes defines the process to be explained;
- a general statement to introduce the subject;
- a series of logical steps explaining the process – paragraph breaks indicating significant stages;
- a final sentence summarising the explanation, and answering the question;
- diagrams to illustrate the explanation.

Annotate the enlarged copy of the text as you identify each feature using Sheet A as your reference.

When you have completed that, tell the children that in the next lesson they will be learning about some more features (linguistic) of explanatory texts.

Now, move on to explain the independent work you would like the children to complete in this lesson. Organise them into mixed ability groups and give them each a copy of Sheet C (or display it on an OHP). Tell them that you want them to read through each example and decide whether they think it is a good explanation text. They should realise straightaway that some of these texts are not so good!

In order to help them, write the following questions on the board for them to think about:

Does the title tell you what is to be explained?

Are technical words used and if so are they explained?

Is the explanation in a clear sequence or is it in a muddle?

How are paragraphs used? What are the sentences like? Short or long?

Is the explanation understandable or is irrelevant or misleading information included?

Ask the children to jot down their ideas and be prepared to feed back their observations in the plenary. Explain that from their observations you are going to draw up a checklist of a good explanation text.

Sit with a group and complete the task. Give the other groups regular time checks ('*Ten minutes left!*') so that they have a chance to consider all the examples.

Plenary

Take feedback from the groups of children and discuss the strengths and weaknesses of the samples. For example, Example 1 does not include a definition of a gas and it includes unnecessary detail about atoms.

Draw up a checklist of what a good explanation should have:

- a title stating what the explanation is about;
- technical words with definitions;
- explanation of how things work in a clear, logical sequence, possibly in time order;
- only relevant information;
- short, clear sentences;
- paragraphs to organise the explanation.

The checklist will be a useful resource for when the children come to write their own explanation texts.

Revving up

Learning objectives

■ To identify the key linguistic features of an explanation text.

■ To understand the use of connectives, causal and sequential, and their impact in linking sentences.

Resources

■ Sheet A (page 71)

■ Collection of explanation texts of the 'how it works' type

■ Sticky notes, A3 paper, felt-tipped pens

What to do

Begin by asking the children to recall the structural features of explanation texts that they identified in the last lesson.

Display an enlarged copy of Sheet A with the annotated features covered up with sticky notes. Ask the children to identify the structural features and, as they do so, reveal the annotated notes from under the sticky notes.

Once they have identified all the structural features, move on to explain that they are now going to look again at the text to find out about other features of explanation texts.

Ask for volunteers to read sections of the text aloud to the rest of the class. After each section, ask a question that prompts the children to identify a particular linguistic feature. For example, read the introduction and focus on the use of verbs. Ask questions such as: *'Who can find a verb in this paragraph?'*, *'Come and underline the verb in the text,'*, *'What tense is the verb?'* and *'Are all the verbs in the text in the same tense?'*

Draw the children's attention to paragraph 3. Ask why most of the verbs here are in the past tense. (Because it is describing the history of the tea bag.)

Move on to read the explanation paragraphs and this time focus on the use of technical vocabulary and connectives. Ask questions such as:

'What does the word "extract" mean?', 'Why has the author used that word?', 'How has the author made sure we understand the word?', 'Can you find any other examples of technical language used in the text?'

'Look at the word "then"; what kind of word is it?', 'Can you find another example of a connective?', 'Let's go back to "then". Is it a sequential or causal connective?', 'Sequential means it helps to tell you that this is a sequence of events, it tells you what happens next. Can you think of any other examples of sequential connectives?' (next, now, when) *'Causal means it tells you what happens as the result of an action.'* (because, this means, since)

Continue through the text in this way, highlighting the linguistic features as shown on the annotated text and listed below:

• written in the present tense because it is a general and repeated process;

• generalised participants, written in the third person;

• sequential connectives (such as when…, then) help to indicate the stages in the sequence;

• causal connectives (such as if/then, so, as a consequence, since);

• technical terminology.

Reveal the annotations on the enlarged copy of the text as you identify each linguistic feature.

Next, explain what you would like the children to do for their independent work. Tell them that you want them to collect and categorise different connectives used in explanation texts.

Give them several explanation texts from leaflets or books to look at in groups of two or three. Ask them to identify the connectives in the explanations and write them in two groups on the A3 piece of paper: those to do with time (sequential) and those to do with cause and effect (causal). Circulate round the groups making sure they understand the difference between sequential and causal connectives.

Plenary

Ask each group of children to join with another group and compare their answers for a few minutes. Have they found any different connectives? Have they categorised the connectives in the same way?

Then ask the groups to feed back. As they do so, check that the connectives are correctly identified and categorised and make a class list. The list will be a useful resource for when the children come to write their own explanations.

Finish the lesson by asking each group to invent a sentence using some of the words and phrases on the list. Can they use a connective at the beginning of a sentence and in the middle of the sentence? Give them five minutes and then ask them to read out their sentence. Write up their sentence on the board as they do so. Ask one person from the group to circle the connectives.

Examples of connectives to do with time:

before, later, next, after, then, just then, almost immediately, as soon as possible.

Examples of connectives to do with cause and effect:

because, so, this causes, consequently, as a result, this makes, as, since.

Taking off

Learning objectives

■ To compile a flow chart to illustrate the processes of freezing water and melting ice.

■ To write the opening general statement of an explanation text.

Resources

■ Sheet B (page 72) and Sheet D (page 74)

■ Sticky notes, A3 paper

What to do

Tell the children that today they are going to begin writing their own explanation text on 'How can you turn water into ice?' Explain that a good way to plan the explanation is to use a diagram that includes the information you want to use. (Diagrams to illustrate explanation texts can take the form of brainstorms, mind maps or flow charts depending on the process they are illustrating. The water cycle can be illustrated on a flow chart. Magnetism can be described on a mind map or brainstorm.)

Tell them that before they do this, they are going to draw and label a shared diagram as a class.

Remind the children about the tea bag explanation (Sheet B). Tell them that you are going to show them how to do a mind map diagram to accompany this text.

Write the phrase 'tea bag' in the centre of the board and ask the children to work in twos and threes to brainstorm all the words and phrases they can think of to do with how a tea bag works. Ask them to list the words on a piece of paper or mini whiteboard.

Ask a couple of volunteers to read out their lists and then start to draw and label the diagram. As you do so, think aloud to model gathering your ideas for the children. For example, you could say:

'I need information about tea, tea bags and making tea so I am going to write the words "tea", "teabag", "paper", "cloth", "boiling water", "cup", "milk and sugar" and "spoon". The title of my diagram is 'How does a tea bag work?' so I need to describe what tea bags are like. Well, they are different shapes and are made from cloth or paper. As you talk write the labels and draw the lines linking the different aspects (see below) to complete the diagram.

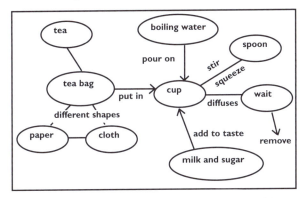

When the diagram is finished, discuss with the children the sorts of words you have used as labels. They are generally nouns or verbs. Also discuss the lines and arrows you have used and what they mean.

Ask for a volunteer to explain how a tea bag works as if they were talking to someone on the telephone. Hide the diagram you have just created. Let the volunteer explain away for a few minutes and then discuss with the children how much easier it is to explain something and understand an explanation when you can see a diagram.

Tell them that, for their independent work, you would like them to work in groups of two or three to draw their own diagrams describing the process of how water can be turned into ice. Explain that this will help them to write their explanation texts.

Start them off by telling them to write the title of the explanation, 'How can you turn water into ice?' Then, they need to brainstorm all the words and phrases they can think of to describe the process and finally they can draw their diagram. Answer any queries and send the children off to complete their work.

After five minutes, stop all the groups to take feedback, answer any queries and ensure everyone is on the right track. Give them time to complete their diagrams.

The diagrams need to be checked before the next lesson in order to correct any misunderstandings the children might have. (See below for an example.)

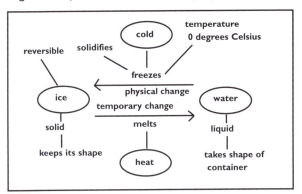

Plenary

Share some of the diagrams. Tell the children that they are going to use their diagrams in the next lesson to help them write their explanation text.

Explain that you are now going to write the opening statement of the explanation together. Write the title on a blank writing frame (Sheet D) and begin to write the introductory paragraph. As you write, think aloud so that the children can hear and see the process.

For example, ask *'What is the purpose of the opening paragraph?'* (A general statement introducing the subject which the explanation is about.) *'What information do you think we should put in this paragraph?'* Take two or three suggestions and then write something along the lines of:

All materials can be put into three groups: solids, liquids and gases. Water can be a solid, a liquid or a gas. Ice is the solid form of water, water is the liquid form of water and water vapour is the gaseous form. The form that water takes depends upon temperature. (Temperature tells us how hot or cold things are.)

Answer any queries and then send the children off to individually write their opening paragraphs on their writing frames. Encourage them to keep their introductions brief. Give them five minutes and then ask for several volunteers to read out their work. Comment on the good points and ways the work could be improved.

Finish by explaining that in the next lesson the children will write the rest of their explanation texts using their diagrams for guidance.

Flying solo

Learning objective

■ To write an explanation text.

Resources

■ Sheet A (page 71)

■ Sheet D (page 74), an enlarged version with the title and opening statement filled in from previous lesson and children's own copy of the page

■ The children's own diagrams from previous lesson

■ List of connectives from 'Revving up'

What to do

Display the class list of connectives and Sheet A for reference as the children write their own explanations.

Put up the enlarged copy of the writing frame with the title and opening paragraph completed from the previous lesson. Ask for a volunteer to read through the opening paragraph of the explanation in order to remind the children of the question they are answering.

Tell them that they are now going to finish their explanation text by writing the explanatory paragraphs and the conclusion, using their diagrams to help them.

To set them off on the right track, ask them to tell you what they think they are going to say in their explanatory paragraphs to answer the question 'How can you turn water into ice?' Listen to a number of suggestions and then jot down in the paragraph boxes on the writing frame the basic gist of each paragraph. For example:

paragraph 1– general properties of water as a liquid – good for dissolving materials in; can be in the shape of droplets;

paragraph 2 – freezing – water can be changed by cooling it; physical change called freezing; properties of water as ice; freezes at 0° Celsius; definition of freezing; expands when it freezes; ice floats; water changes how it looks and feels; temporary change that can be reversed by heat; reversal is called melting;

paragraph 3 – melting – ice can be changed back to water by heating it; freezing is a temporary change; solid to liquid; melting; properties of melting.

As you make the notes, highlight the linguistic features listed on the frame to remind the children to use them. Answer any queries they might have and then send them off to start their task.

After about ten minutes, stop the class in order to demonstrate the writing of the conclusion. Ask, 'What is the purpose of a conclusion?' (to summarise the answer to the question or the explanation). Ask the children for suggestions of what they might say in the conclusion. Take two or three responses and then talk through the conclusion encouraging them to help with forming the ideas and constructing the sentences. For example:

> *When you cool a liquid it changes to a solid. If you freeze water at 0° Celsius it solidifies to make ice. This is a physical change of state and can be reversed. If you heat ice it melts and becomes water again.*

Ask the children to finish their explanations.

Plenary

Ask for two or three children to read out their explanations, one to read the opening statement, the next the explanatory paragraphs and the last the conclusion. Ask the rest of the class to point out examples of the key linguistic features of explanation texts, for example: any technical terminology used and explained, examples of causal connectives, present tense verbs, action verbs and sequential connectives.

Finish the lesson by reflecting with the children on what they have learned about the structure of writing explanation texts. Some areas for discussion could be:

• opening general statement;

• use of paragraphs;

• use of diagrams to enhance explanations;

• a conclusion.

How does a tea bag work?

opening general statement

Tea is the world's most popular beverage. From Russia to southern Africa...from America to the Far East...tea is enjoyed in endless different ways.

title – a question requiring an explanation

But all varieties of tea still come from the same plant, *Camellia sinensis*. The tea plant flourishes with plentiful rain, acid soils, and specific seasonal variations in temperature.

sub heading

The Chinese have been drinking tea for the last 5,000 years but tea bags are said to have been created by accident about 50 years ago. A New York tea importer named Thomas Sullivan sent samples of tea to his customers in small silk bags. The customers liked the convenience of having their tea in silk bags because they were soon requesting all their tea in bagged form.

third person

What is a tea bag?
A tea bag is a cloth or paper bag holding enough tea for an individual serving of a drink of tea. The tea bag is soaked in water, which has previously been boiled, to extract, that is draw out, the full flavour of the tea.

diagrams to clarify and add meaning

How to make a perfect cup of tea
In order to make the perfect cup of tea you need to boil fresh water. Make sure you boil the water to more than 98.5 degrees centigrade so that the flavour from the tea leaves can be extracted.

use of technical terms

Then, pour the water onto the bag in the cup and leave it to brew for a few minutes.

To help this brewing process, squeeze the teabag against the side of the cup with a spoon for several seconds. Stir the tea once and then squeeze the bag again for a further few seconds.

sequential connective

Finally, remove the tea bag from the cup. Milk should be added last, otherwise it will lower the temperature and affect the brewing process. Add sugar, as required.

present tense

A tea bag works by acting as a filter allowing the tea flavour to flood out into the water and, consequently, makes a new solution, tea! Because the tea bag is a filter, the tea leaves are left behind as the residue.

causal connective

conclusion

Now that you know how a tea bag works, have a break and make yourself a cuppa!

How does a tea bag work?

Tea is the world's most popular beverage. From Russia to southern Africa...from America to the Far East...tea is enjoyed in endless different ways.

But all varieties of tea still come from the same plant, Camellia sinensis. The tea plant flourishes with plentiful rain, acid soils, and specific seasonal variations in temperature.

The Chinese have been drinking tea for the last 5,000 years but tea bags are said to have been created by accident about 50 years ago. A New York tea importer named Thomas Sullivan sent samples of tea to his customers in small silk bags. The customers liked the convenience of having their tea in silk bags because they were soon requesting all their tea in bagged form.

What is a tea bag?

A tea bag is a cloth or paper bag holding enough tea for an individual serving of a drink of tea. The tea bag is soaked in water, which has previously been boiled, to extract, that is draw out, the full flavour of the tea.

How to make a perfect cup of tea

In order to make the perfect cup of tea you need to boil fresh water. Make sure you boil the water to more than 98.5 degrees centigrade so that the flavour from the tea leaves can be extracted.

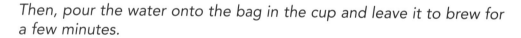

Then, pour the water onto the bag in the cup and leave it to brew for a few minutes.

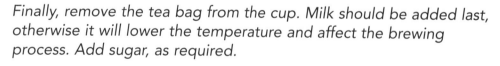

To help this brewing process, squeeze the tea bag against the side of the cup with a spoon for several seconds. Stir the tea once and then squeeze the bag again for a further few seconds.

Finally, remove the tea bag from the cup. Milk should be added last, otherwise it will lower the temperature and affect the brewing process. Add sugar, as required.

A tea bag works by acting as a filter allowing the tea flavour to flood out into the water and consequently, makes a new solution, tea! Because the tea bag is a filter, the tea leaves are left behind as the residue.

Now that you know how a tea bag works, have a break and make yourself a cuppa!

Sheet C

Example 1: The properties of solids and liquids

There are three states of matter – solid, liquid and gas. Each state has particular characteristics to do with the way the particles that make up a material are arranged and behave. Everything is made up of particles: particles can be single atoms or groups of atoms. Atoms have a nucleus made of protons and neutrons; electrons surround the nucleus. Solids have a fixed size and shape, which generally only changes if they are acted upon by something else. Liquids have volume – they take up a certain amount of space – but they don't have a definite shape, instead taking up the shape of whatever contains them.

Example 3: Solids and liquids

There are lots of different solids and lots of different liquids. Water is a liquid – so are apple juice, orange squash, Coke, lemonade and cranberry juice. You can drink many liquids. Wood is a solid – so are a knife, an apple and a cup. You can't eat all solids.

There are lots of gases, too. Gases are all around us. You cannot see them because they are invisible. Oxygen is a gas.

Example 2: What are the differences between solids and liquids?

All materials can be put into three groups: solids, liquids or gases. All materials are made up of very small particles held together by forces.

Solids, such as a metal spoon, a brick or a chunk of cheese, are easy to control. All the particles in solids are packed tightly together and can hardly move.

Liquids, such as water or apple juice, are more difficult to control. The particles in liquids are not so tightly packed and can move a little.

Solids keep their shape while liquids are runny. Solids can be cut or shaped. Liquids take up the shape of any container.

Solids and liquids have different properties. Solids are easy to control – you can take hold of a solid. Liquids are more difficult to control – they keep wanting to run away.

Example 4: Solids and liquids – is there a difference?

Solids are tightly packed together and cannot move. They are solid.

Liquids are not packed together so closely. They are runny.

You can wash yourself with soap, which is a solid.

You can drink water, which is a liquid.

Solids and liquids are different.

Sheet D

Writing
across the
Curriculum

Title

Opening statement

> What are you going to explain?

Explanation

Paragraph 1 – general information

> Explain how things work in a clear sequence.

Paragraph 2 – information about freezing

> Use and explain technical terms.

Paragraph 3 – information about melting

> Use connectives such as: because, this means that, this makes, therefore, consequently, next, because of this, as a result.

Conclusion

> Write a summary to answer the question in the title.

Unit 2

Lesson focus

Geography Unit 9 – Village settlers

Overall aim

To identify the features of an explanation text and to write an explanation about early village settlers.

Geography emphasis

This unit introduces the children to settlements: how they have developed over time and how early settlers established many of our settlements that exist today. They will use geographical enquiry skills, maps and geographical terms.

Literacy links

Year 4, Term 2: T19, T20, T24, T25, S4

About this unit

Geography Unit 9 'Village settlers' combines work from the History Scheme of Work on Romans, Anglo-Saxons and Vikings in Britain. It can be used as a geographical study within a history unit or later to revisit work previously completed in history.

The lessons outlined here can be taught in literacy sessions alongside the geography unit. Literacy work links to the first couple of sections of the geography unit of work.

Switching on

Learning objectives

- To read, enjoy and understand an explanation text.
- To identify the key structural features of an explanation text.
- To understand the functions of paragraphs.

Resources

- Sheets A to C (pages 80 to 82)

What to do

Introduce the explanation text on settlements (Sheet B) to the children by asking them to recall the work they are doing in geography on village settlers linked to whichever history unit (Romans, Vikings or Anglo-Saxons) you have selected.

Explain that they are going to learn more about the special features of explanation texts and then write an explanation about early village settlers, using the information they have been finding in geography and history.

Read the shared text to the children. As you read, check their understanding of the content of the text through

questioning and make sure they understand all the vocabulary used. Ask for volunteers to look up unknown words in a dictionary and clarify the meanings of any difficult words.

Then ask the children 'Who might use this text and why?' (People who want to find out about settlements, but who do not know much about the topic.)

Involve the class in rereading the text, paying particular attention to the structural features. For example, stop after the first two paragraphs and ask 'What can you tell me about the title of this explanation text?' (It is asking a question, which will be answered in the text.) 'Do all explanation texts ask a question in the title?' (No; some have titles which define the process to be explained.) 'What does the first paragraph of the text tell us?' Listen to a few responses and then agree with the children that it sets the scene to introduce the topic of settlements. It tells us general things about settlements.

Continue through the text, highlighting the structural features (use Sheet A as your guide):

series of logical steps explaining the concepts – paragraph breaks indicating significant stages;

final sentences summarising the explanation, and answering the question.

When you have completed that, tell the children that in the next lesson they will be identifying other features of this explanation text (the key linguistic features).

Next ask them to tell you what they think a paragraph is. Take a few responses and agree that a paragraph is a section of a piece of writing. It contains sentences about the same subject. Ask them to give reasons why paragraphs are used in writing. Again take a few responses and agree that a new paragraph marks a change of focus, a change of time, a change of place or a change of speaker in a passage of dialogue.

Discuss how a new paragraph is shown and agree that paragraphing helps writers to organise their thoughts and helps readers to follow the text more easily.

Tell the children that they are now going to summarise the information in each paragraph of the shared text into a title and a sentence. Read the first paragraph and ask what it is about. (It defines what a settlement actually is.) Agree a title for the paragraph, such as 'settlements'.

Continue through the text discussing the purpose of each paragraph and deciding on summarising titles. Explain that these titles could be used in the text as subheadings.

Then, explain that for their independent work you want them to read an explanation text, give each paragraph of the text a title and then summarise what it is saying in a short sentence. Provide pairs of children with the sample explanation (Exercise 1 on Sheet C) and ask them to work together on the text. More able children could work on Exercise 2, putting the text into paragraphs first before writing a summative title for each paragraph and a sentence saying what the paragraph is about.

Plenary

Ask the more able pairs to identify where the paragraphs should be in the text first of all. Then work through the text asking for suggestions on the purpose of each paragraph and a summative title. Suggestions for summative titles could be:

- settlements with special functions;
- market towns;
- seaside resorts;
- cities;
- land use in a city;
- where people live in a city.

Share the children's sentences describing what the paragraphs are saying – are they all agreed? What did they find easy or difficult about this task? How has it helped them understand what a paragraph is?

Revving up

Learning objectives

■ To identify the key linguistic features of an explanation text.

■ To brainstorm and collect notes about early settlements.

Resources

■ Sheet A (page 80)

■ Sticky notes, A3 paper, felt-tipped pens

What to do

Display an enlarged version of Sheet A with the annotated features covered up with sticky notes. Ask the children if they can remember the key structural features identified in the text in the previous lesson. Recap these features and uncover each sticky note as you go.

Explain that they are now going to look again at the text to find out about the other features of explanation texts. Involve the class in rereading the shared text. After each paragraph, stop and identify any key linguistic features:

- written in the present tense;
- generalised participants, written in the third person;
- sequential connectives (such as when..., then) help to indicate the stages in the sequence;
- causal connectives (such as if/then, so, as a consequence, since);
- technical terminology.

For example, ask a child to read the first two paragraphs and focus the children's attention on the verbs. Ask for a volunteer to underline all the verbs in the paragraphs. Select a verb and ask: *'What tense is that verb? Is the tense the same throughout?'*

Select another child to read the paragraph about hamlets and focus on the connectives. Revise the different types of connectives – cause and effect or sequential. Ask them to identify other examples of connectives in the text.

Continue through the text, highlighting the linguistic features in this way, uncovering the sticky notes as you go. Tell the children that these are the special features of explanation texts and that they will need to use them when they are writing their own explanation texts.

Next, explain that they are now going to brainstorm and collect information about early village settlers to use in their explanation texts. Tell them they need to be prepared to present their work in the plenary session.

Begin by asking what they already know about early settlers. Ask them to tell their neighbour two things they know. Give them a few minutes to do this and then take two or three answers from them.

Split the class into groups of three or four and give each group a blank sheet of A3 paper and coloured pens. Ask them to start by writing the title of their explanation text in the centre of their paper: 'Why were (name three settlements here) attractive sites for early settlers?' (Relate this to the history unit you have worked on as a class. You may want to tell the children the names of the three settlements or ask them to choose themselves.)

Explain that you want them to brainstorm reasons why these sites were chosen – on top of a hill for defence, near a river for water and so on. Tell them to refer to their work completed in geography and history. Circulate round all the groups, making sure they understand what to do.

Plenary

Ask the groups to present their brainstorms. Each group could select one settlement and give several reasons for early settlement. Allow the other groups the chance to add new information to their brainstorms.

Explain to the children that in the next lesson they will be starting to write their explanation using these brainstorms as a starting point.

Taking off

Learning objectives

■ To write up brainstorm notes on a writing frame.

■ To write the opening general statement of an explanation text.

Resources

■ Sheet D (page 83)

■ Brainstorms from 'Revving up'

■ Map of the chosen settlement areas

What to do

Tell the children that they are now going to begin to write their explanation texts. Say that they are going to use a writing frame and their brainstorms to help them.

Show them an enlarged version of Sheet D. Write the title 'Why were (the three settlement names) attractive sites for early settlers?' on it. Explain that they will begin with the explanation paragraphs first (because this is the information contained in their brainstorms) and then go on to write the introductory paragraph afterwards.

As you write, think aloud so that the children can hear and see the process. The text in italics is what you say out loud as if to yourself; the text in bold is what you write. For example:

I need to write the explanation paragraphs – that is to list the settlements and the reasons why the Romans/Vikings/ Anglo-Saxons settled there. Can anyone give me the name of a settlement?

(Locate it on a map.) Then, encourage the children to give you the reasons for the settlement by referring to their brainstorms and make notes in one of the boxes. For example:

Sowerby, in North Yorkshire, is an example of a Viking village settlement. Let's find Sowerby on the map. Have a look at what is around and near the village site. Who can now give me a reason why the Vikings selected this site? It is located on flat land. What would this have been used for? (Farmland, grazing animals and growing crops.) Who can think of another reason? (It is near the Cod Beck and that would have provided the Vikings with fresh water supplies.) So I am going to write the following words in the first explanation paragraph box on Sheet D **Sowerby, North Yorkshire, flat land, farmland, grazing animals, growing crops, Cod Beck, fresh water supplies.**

Tell the children that you want them to use their own brainstorms to do their own notes on the writing frame. Provide them each with a copy of Sheet D. Work with a group requiring support by writing up the notes on the frame together.

Give them ten minutes or so and then ask them to stop so that you can show them how to go about writing up the opening statement. Ask what they think the purpose of an opening paragraph is. Take a few suggestions and agree with the children that you need to introduce your subject and then make some general points which will be elaborated on in the explanation paragraphs.

As with the explanation paragraphs, show the children how to make notes for the introduction, thinking aloud as you do so. For example:

I want to explain why the Romans/Vikings/Anglo-Saxons settled in these sites. In my opening statement I want to set the scene to answer the question. What can I write? Take suggestions from the children and write, for example, the following words in the opening statement box. **Vikings, from Scandinavia, mostly farmers, sailed all around Europe, longships, 865, great army invaded, fierce battles for several years, Vikings conquered all of northern, central and eastern England, settlements ending in 'by' or 'thorp'.**

Next, talk through these notes, encouraging the children to help with constructing the sentences. For example:

The Vikings invaded England in the eighth century, sailing their longships, long open warships which were propelled by oars and a sail, across the North Sea from Scandinavia. They began settling on land across northern, central and eastern England in

AD865, on sites suitable for farming and grazing their livestock.

As you are writing the sentences out, discuss the verb tense and explain that the past tense is used because they are writing about something that has already happened.

Ask the children to finish making notes on their writing frame for the introduction and the explanation paragraphs and then use the notes to write their opening paragraphs of their explanation text.

Plenary

Ask several children to read out their opening statements. Discuss their good points as a class:

- general statement about Romans/Vikings/Anglo-Saxons;

- past tense used – remind the children that past tense is used in historical explanations;

- technical terminology explained.

Finish by asking the children to share their opening statement with a partner to help with any grammatical or spelling errors which need correcting. Allow time for the corrections to be made.

Flying solo

Learning objective

■ To write an explanation text.

Resources

■ Sheet D (page 83)

■ A collection of non-fiction texts and leaflets, some of which include explanations

What to do

Begin the lesson by asking volunteers to read out their opening paragraphs in order to set the scene for the completion of the explanation texts.

Now, demonstrate the writing of the next paragraph, talking through the process of composing and revising sentences in the head. Display the enlarged writing frame you partially completed in the previous lesson and tell the children you are now going to do some shared writing of an explanation paragraph. Think aloud as you plan and write your paragraph. Again, the italic text is what you say and the bold text is what you write.

I'll just look at my writing frame notes for writing my first paragraph. My first site is the village of Sowerby. Now, what were the Vikings' reasons for choosing this site? Because it was on flat land and near water. So, I'm going to write **Sowerby in North Yorkshire is one example of a Viking village settlement.** *Explanations are about giving reasons why things happen so a good way to start a sentence would be 'One reason for … so what about',* **One reason for this was that it is located near the Cod Beck, which would have provided the Vikings with fresh water supplies?** *Let me read that back to you. It is good but I think we need to say why the Vikings needed fresh water supplies.* **The Vikings needed fresh water for drinking, cooking, washing and their livestock.**

Tell the children it is now their turn to write. Answer any queries and send them away to write their explanation paragraphs of their explanation text. Give them time to complete or nearly complete the task and then regroup them in order to demonstrate the writing of the conclusion.

Remind them that the function of a conclusion is to reiterate the answer to the question posed in the title of the explanation. Ask them to give you some suggestions for the answer to the question. Take a few suggestions and then agree that in their explanation text the answer to the question is the reasons why the early settlers chose the villages. Some of these reasons could be, for example, 'easy to defend' and 'close to a water supply'.

Ask the children to work in pairs to make up a concluding sentence, or sentences, orally or to write on a small whiteboard. Encourage them to read their sentences out loud to each other in order to identify any mistakes. Then, share some of their sentences, choosing some and making changes where necessary and saying why you chose to use these sentences. Then read them back to the children. The concluding paragraph could be something like:

> *The Vikings settled mainly in the north, centre and east of England. They chose sites for their villages that were easy to defend, near fresh water supplies and on flat farmland so that they could grow crops and graze their livestock.*

Point out the use of the causal connective 'so' and ask the children to check their explanation texts to make sure they have used several examples of connectives in their writing. Then, send them off to write the conclusions for their reports. The explanations can be completed with pictures and maps after they have been proofread and the spellings checked.

Plenary

Ask the children to work in pairs to look through a range of texts and leaflets and choose one that they think is an example of an explanation text. Ask how they knew it was an explanation text. Give the pairs time to work out several reasons why they think it is an explanation text and then take feedback.

Points for discussion include: structural features – title, paragraphs, diagrams and conclusion; linguistic features – sequential and time and cause connectives, technical terminology, verbs and tenses.

Writing across the **Curriculum**

What is a settlement?

opening general statement

title – a question requiring an explanation

A settlement is a place where people live and work. Settlements are usually permanent; as a result people have lived in these places for a long time. There are different types of settlements: farms, hamlets, villages, towns and cities.

use of technical terms

Farms are usually found in the countryside because they consist of several fields. They are the smallest type of settlement, usually with a farmhouse and farm buildings. Most farms will have an electricity and water supply and telephone and postal services.

Hamlets are small groups of houses. A hamlet does not have its own church or shops, so people who live in hamlets have to go to other settlements for things like food and clothes.

paragraph breaks indicating stages

causal connective

After a hamlet, a village is next in size. It is bigger than a hamlet. You find villages in rural settings. They have many houses with more people living there. Most villages have a bus service, shops and sometimes a post office, although village post offices are on the decline now. There may be a church and a village hall where people can meet. There will probably be a primary school and a park.

third person

Next is a town. A town is larger than a village but smaller than a city. Towns have many more shops selling things that you can't buy in villages, such as clothes, furniture and electrical goods. A town has primary and secondary schools, garages, health centres and a town hall. There are places to eat and leisure facilities like cinemas and sports centres and there may be a railway station.

sequential connective

Finally, a city is a town that has received the title of 'City' from the Crown and is usually the seat of a bishop, so it has a cathedral. There may be hundreds of thousands of people living in a city. Consequently, the city centre has lots of different kinds of shops and forms of entertainment for them. A city usually has a hospital and there may be a university and an airport on the outskirts.

present tense

A settlement is a place where people live and work. It can be small, like a farm with only several people living there or very large, like a city with hundreds of thousands of people living and working there.

conclusion

What is a settlement?

A settlement is a place where people live and work. Settlements are usually permanent; as a result people have lived in these places for a long time. There are different types of settlements: farms, hamlets, villages, towns and cities.

Farms are usually found in the countryside because they consist of several fields. They are the smallest type of settlement, usually with a farmhouse and farm buildings. Most farms will have an electricity and water supply and telephone and postal services.

Hamlets are small groups of houses. A hamlet does not have its own church or shops, so people who live in hamlets have to go to other settlements for things like food and clothes.

After a hamlet, a village is next in size. It is bigger than a hamlet. You find villages in rural settings. They have many houses with more people living there. Most villages have a bus service, shops and sometimes a post office, although village post offices are on the decline now. There may be a church and a village hall where people can meet. There will probably be a primary school and a park.

Next is a town. A town is larger than a village but smaller than a city. Towns have many more shops selling things that you can't buy in villages, such as clothes, furniture and electrical goods. A town has primary and secondary schools, garages, health centres and a town hall. There are places to eat and leisure facilities like cinemas and sports centres and there may be a railway station.

Finally, a city is a town that has received the title of 'City' from the Crown and is usually the seat of a bishop, so it has a cathedral. There may be hundreds of thousands of people living in a city. Consequently, the city centre has lots of different kinds of shops and forms of entertainment for them. A city usually has a hospital and there may be a university and an airport on the outskirts.

A settlement is a place where people live and work. It can be small, like a farm with only several people living there or very large, like a city with hundreds of thousands of people living and working there.

Sheet C

Exercise 1

Settlements occur because people need places to live and work. Some settlements have special functions because of what happens in them. Here are some examples.

Market towns are places where farmers and other local people would have taken goods to sell in the past. Some towns still have a market place where local people may take goods to sell.

People like going on holiday by the sea because of the sea, the sand and, hopefully, the sun. These places are called seaside resorts and are dotted around the coast. Some seaside towns have sandy beaches, fish and chip shops and amusement arcades. Other seaside resorts have a rocky shore with rockpools to fish in or an old fishing port and fishing trawlers.

Cities are another type of settlement. If you walk or drive through a city, you can see lots of different things: houses, blocks of flats, shops, offices, factories, parks for walking and playing, roads and railways.

Not many people actually live in the city centre. Most of the buildings there are shops, offices and public buildings like museums and halls. Some people live in flats in city centres. Most people live in residential areas called estates, just outside the city centre.

The area around the city centre is called the inner city. The houses are often arranged in terraces. Terraced houses were first built at the beginning of the twentieth century. They were small and often did not have toilets and bathrooms inside, so lots of them could be built. Today, these houses have been improved or replaced by blocks of flats.

Exercise 2

Settlements occur because people need places to live and work. Some settlements have special functions because of what happens in them. Here are some examples. Market towns are places where farmers and other local people would have taken goods to sell in the past. Some towns still have a market place where local people may take goods to sell. People like going on holiday by the sea because of the sea, the sand and, hopefully, the sun. These places are called seaside resorts and are dotted around the coast. Some seaside towns have sandy beaches, fish and chip shops and amusement arcades. Other seaside resorts have a rocky shore with rockpools to fish in or an old fishing port and fishing trawlers. Cities are another type of settlement. If you walk or drive through a city, you can see lots of different things: houses, blocks of flats, shops, offices, factories, parks for walking and playing, roads and railways. Not many people actually live in the city centre. Most of the buildings there are shops, offices and public buildings like museums and halls. Some people live in flats in city centres. Most people live in residential areas called estates, just outside the city centre. The area around the city centre is called the inner city. The houses are often arranged in terraces. Terraced houses were first built at the beginning of the twentieth century. They were small and often did not have toilets and bathrooms inside, so lots of them could be built. Today, these houses have been improved or replaced by blocks of flats.

Sheet D

Title

Opening statement: I want to explain why...

Explanation – paragraph 1

paragraph 2

paragraph 3

Conclusion

Chapter 5

Persuasion writing

What is a persuasion text?

A persuasion text argues the case for a belief or issue from a particular point of view. The point of view is supported by evidence and reasoning.

Structural features

- Usually begins with an opening statement to indicate the point of view to be expressed
- Main body of text lists the arguments for the point of view supported by evidence and reasoning
- Ends with a conclusion that reiterates the opening statement and presents a summary of the arguments presented

Linguistic features

- Present tense
- General terms used (such as 'people should' rather than 'Mr Jones should')

- Use of connectives to show logic (therefore, however, because of, due to, despite, this shows, in spite of, as a result of)
- Often uses rhetorical questions addressed directly to the reader (Can you believe?)
- Alliterative sentences (in advertisements especially)
- Emotive and persuasive language
- Use of pictures/illustrations to gain an emotional response from the reader

Examples of persuasion texts

- advertisements
- travel brochures
- letters to express a point of view
- propaganda leaflets
- newspaper or magazine articles

Teaching persuasion writing

It is incredibly easy for children to express their opinions but giving reasons for these opinions is not so simple! Children need lots of oral practice in determining the reasons behind their opinions before they can begin to write them.

When writing persuasively children need to know their subject well and be able to provide supporting evidence (facts or believable fiction) as well as predicting any possible counter-arguments. It is vital that they have lots of opportunities to read examples of persuasive writing in order to be able to identify the features and evaluate the success of different persuasive devices before actually trying them out themselves.

The purpose of the text is of the utmost importance. What does the writer want the reader to do in response? Having a clear idea of the proposed outcome will ensure the children experience more successful planning and completion of the writing.

Persuasion writing – progression

Persuasive texts are introduced in Year 3 through letter writing (Term 3: T16).

In **Year 4** children read, compare and evaluate examples of arguments, look at how arguments are presented and how statistics and graphs can be used to support arguments and investigate how style and vocabulary are used to convince the reader (Term 3: T16, T17, T18). They assemble and sequence points in order to plan the presentation of a point of view, using writing frames to back up points of view with illustrations and examples and to present the point of view in the form of a letter, script or report (Term 3: T21, T22, T23). They evaluate adverts for their impact, appeal and honesty and design their own (Term 3: T19, T25).

In Year 5 children read and evaluate letters intended to persuade. They collect and investigate persuasive devices. They write letters for real issues, write commentaries on an issue and construct and present an argument to the class (Term 3: T12, T14, T15, T17, T18, T19).

In Year 6 they look at how effective arguments are made and make one themselves (Term 2: T15, T16, T18).

Unit 1

Lesson focus

Geography Unit 8 – Improving the environment

Overall aim

To write a persuasive text in the form of a letter to the headteacher on how to improve the school grounds and buildings.

Geography emphasis

In this unit children will learn about local environmental issues using their school, the grounds and the immediate neighbourhood. They will develop a respect for the environment and evaluate their own and others' effect on it and will be encouraged to become actively involved in improving their local environment.

Literacy links

Year 4, Term 3: T19, T25, S2, S4

About this unit

In order to write a persuasion text, children need to be knowledgeable about the subject concerned. In this unit they are given the opportunity to develop, express and justify their opinions through role play and discussion of how to improve their school. This focus on discussion needs to be a continuous part of the writing process.

It is useful if the children have already had some experience of investigating the school and local neighbourhood, such as in Geography Unit 6 'Investigating the Local Area' and have begun to develop a range of geographical concepts.

Switching on

Learning objectives

■ To identify a range of relevant subjects for persuasive writing.

■ To develop, express and justify opinions through discussion and role play.

Resource

■ A large space for drama activities

What to do

Start the lesson by asking the children a question about their school that is guaranteed to be answered with a range of opinions; for example, 'What do you think about allowing people to play ball games in the playground?'

Listen to a number of answers representing different points of view. As you listen, explain to the children that different opinions represent different points of view. Encourage them to give reasons and examples for their opinions.

Then say 'That question really got you thinking and gave me lots of information about your different opinions.' Tell them that in the next few lessons they are going to think more about their opinions on different issues and that they will be trying to justify what they think. Explain that they are

going to begin by thinking more about their school and its environment. Tell them that you want them to work in pairs to think about ways to improve the school, the grounds and the buildings. Ask them to think especially about the issues that they think people will have different views about, such as what meals should be served in the school canteen, litter, playground equipment, seating in the playground, use of the playing field and parking outside the school at home time.

After five minutes or so, ask each pair to briefly share their ideas. List all the ideas on the board. Tell the children that they are now going to do some drama, freeze-framing. This will help them to choose a topic and develop their ideas in order to write a persuasive text at a later stage. Divide the children into small groups.

First, they need to choose a topic from the list and then spend five minutes or so deciding how they will represent that topic in a freeze-frame. For example, the topic could be litter, and the drama freeze-frame could be: one child is in the act of dropping some litter on the ground, another child is expressing horror at the litter lout, while another child has an accident by cutting herself on some dropped litter. Allow each group time to choose a topic and prepare a freeze-frame. (If the children have not had much experience at freeze-framing, you may need to provide them with a few more examples of how to freeze-frame an issue in order to get them started.)

Ask each group to act out their freeze-frame. Tell them you now want each character to step out of the freeze-frame and comment on their own part in it. For example, the child who dropped the litter could say, '*I couldn't find a bin. We need to have more bins in the playground.*' The child expressing horror might say, '*I am disgusted by the litter lout making the playground look untidy. She needs to stop being selfish and take responsibility for her own actions. She ought to be made to pick up all the litter in the playground.*' The child who has hurt herself could say, '*I would not have cut myself if the litter had been thrown away in a bin. No litter in the playground would mean a safer playground.*'

Give the children ten minutes or so to practise their freeze-frame and the stepping out of character role.

As you work with the groups, challenge them to come up with comments that represent their character's point of view, and then to give reasons and examples to support that point of view. Remember the topics are ways of improving the school.

Plenary

Spend the plenary time with the groups acting out their freeze-frames and then stepping out of character to explain their actions. Encourage the children to challenge each other's opinions by asking for clarification or evidence.

Revving up

Learning objectives

■ To read and evaluate different kinds of persuasive writing.

■ To identify the structural and linguistic features of persuasive texts.

Resources

■ A collection of persuasive texts, such as letters, leaflets, advertisements and posters

■ Sticky notes

What to do

Remind the children about the previous lesson where they thought about a range of issues to do with improving the school and its environment. Tell them that they are going to write a letter to try and persuade their headteacher to make improvements to the school but before they do that they need to learn more about the special features of persuasive texts.

Show the class the collection of persuasive texts. Explain that you want them to choose one of the texts, read it and then identify features of persuasive writing in the text.

To support this analysis, write a list of key points on the board that you want the children to consider:

Purpose – why has the text been written?

Audience – who is going to read the text?

Structure – is there an opening statement? Is the text organised into paragraphs? Is there a conclusion?

Language – what verb tense is it written in? Are adjectives used a lot?

Make sure they understand the terminology before they begin by revising the meaning of terms such as 'introduction', 'conclusion', 'verb' and 'adjective'.

Ask the children to work in twos or threes and to be prepared to share what they have found out about their text with the rest of the class. They could record their findings by writing labels on sticky notes to stick on their text.

Work with a group of children, analysing one example of a persuasive text. Ask them to take it in turns to read the text aloud first; then consider the key points collectively.

Plenary

Organise the groups to present their text and features to the rest of the class and prompt the other children to ask questions about it. You will probably only have time for four or five groups.

Then work together to categorise the examples into:

- form, such as letters, fliers, brochures and advertisements

  and

- purpose, such as to complain, convince or protest.

Next, identify the special features of persuasive texts, as listed below:

- introduction states the point of view;
- language is used to gain reader's attention;
- written in the present tense;
- persuasive devices, such as 'Surely you can see that...';
- emotive language;
- organised as sequence of arguments;
- use of factual evidence to support the point of view;
- use of adjectives;
- use of rhetorical questions;
- linking words make logical connections;
- detail and explanation support the main points;
- presents opinion as fact;
- use of pictures/illustrations;
- conclusion summarises the point of view.

List these features on the board. Ask the children to find examples of different kinds of persuasive writing at home. These could be used in a display.

Taking off

Learning objective

■ To plan a persuasive text using a writing frame.

Resource

■ Sheet A (page 90)

What to do

Display an enlarged version of Sheet A. Explain to the children that they are now going to plan their persuasive text. Tell them that you want them to choose a lively, interesting issue that they feel strongly about from the 'Switching on' lesson when they discussed how to improve the school, its grounds and the buildings. Give them a couple of minutes to discuss with their neighbour which issue they are going to write about.

Ask for a few suggestions and then choose one, such as 'More playground equipment and toys should be provided at lunchtime play.' Write this in the 'Issue to be discussed' section of the writing frame.

Explain that the audience will be their headteacher (write this in the frame) and the form will be a letter (write this in the frame).

Tell the children that you are now going to do some shared writing to show them how to complete the rest of the frame. Following is a script **for your eyes only** which you can use or adapt. The text in italics is what you say out loud as if to yourself; the text in bold is what you write in note form on the frame.

Right, our issue is that we want more playground equipment and toys at lunchtimes, so my first point is this: **With playground equipment like balls, skittles and** *skipping ropes, children can learn to play new games. Now why do I think this? Firstly,* **Because the lunchtime assistants and older children could teach the younger children games to play.** *Another reason is* **Children will be playing together; no-one will be lonely.** *My last reason is that* **With so much to do, the children will behave themselves, making the lunchtime assistants' job easier.**

Move on to complete Points 2 and 3 on the frame by taking suggestions from the children.

Explain that for their independent work you want them to complete their own writing frame. Provide them with their own copies of Sheet A.

It is a good idea to work with a group requiring support at this stage, perhaps completing the writing frame as a group rather than individually.

Plenary

Ask for a volunteer to read out their issue and one of the points from their writing frame, along with the reasons and examples they have stated. Explain that you are now going to show the class how to write persuasively, using some of the features they have previously identified.

So, for example, the issue could be 'using the field at playtime'. The first point might be 'playing ball games on the field' and the reasons and examples might include 'the need for more space' and 'balls injuring children'. Write the following sentence on the board:

> **Children should be allowed to use the playing field at playtime so that they can play football on it.**

Ask for sentence suggestions that explain why football should be played on the field – sentences which justify the statement. Encourage the children to use connectives, adjectives and emotive language. For example:

> **As a result of football being played in the playground by the older boys, there is no room for the younger children to run around. Moreover, children are being injured; they are being knocked down and hit by the hard football. Playtime is becoming extremely dangerous.**

Now, ask the children to think up a rhetorical question (explain what this is – a question for which we don't expect an answer) and further sentences using persuasive words and phrases. For example:

How many children are going to be injured before action is taken? Only last week a child in Year 1 was hit in the face by a football. Surely we are entitled to a safe playtime!

Finish by telling the class that in the next lesson they will be writing their own persuasive sentences.

Flying solo

Learning objectives

■ To write a persuasive letter.

■ To use characteristic features of persuasive writing effectively.

Resource

■ Sheet A (page 90)

What to do

Tell the children they are now going to write their persuasive letter using their notes on the writing frame from the previous lesson.

Explain that you are going to start them off on the right track by doing some shared writing to begin their letters. This will ensure they write their letters in the correct format.

Begin by asking them how they think a formal letter should be set out. *'What goes at the top right of the letter?'* (The writer's address.) *'Where on the page should the recipient's address be written?'* (The left-hand side, a line under where the writer's address finishes.) Demonstrate writing the addresses. Discuss and demonstrate other features, such as where to write the date and how to begin and end the letter.

Ask the children to begin writing their own letter. Work with a group requiring support or enrichment. After ten minutes or so, stop the children and ask for volunteers to read out their work. Highlight the good points for the class to share:

■ each point (from the writing frame) is a new paragraph;

■ the use of connectives;

■ good reasons and arguments and so on.

Give the children time to finish their letters.

Plenary

To round off this series of lessons, pose these big questions about persuasive writing for the children to consider:

■ Is the argument clear? – Are the main points set out clearly? Are ideas clearly and logically linked? Have I used connecting words or phrases? Have I supported my points with reasons and explanations?

■ Is the text well organised? – Is there an effective introduction? Is there an effective conclusion? Are ideas organised in paragraphs? Does each paragraph have a clear focus?

■ How can we improve the work?

Select a couple of children's letters to look at and review as a class.

Choose three or four letters to give to the headteacher. Hopefully a reply will be forthcoming!

Sheet A

Issue to be discussed Audience – who do I want to read my text? Form – how am I going to present my text?	
Point 1	Reasons and examples
Point 2	Reasons and examples
Point 3	Reasons and examples

Unit 2

Lesson focus

Design and Technology Unit 4e – Lighting it up

Overall aim

To design an advertisement on paper or on screen using structural and linguistic features of persuasive texts gathered from reading.

Design and Technology emphasis

In this unit the children apply and reinforce their learning from the 'design and make' section of Unit 4e (where they make a light). They draw a labelled diagram of their light, identifying the key features. When creating their advertisement, they focus on thinking about the needs of the potential user of their light – the potential audience.

Literacy links

Year 4, Term 3: T16, T17, T18, T21, T22, T23, S4

About this unit

In this unit the children are required to design an advertisement for a light they have made in D&T.

The lessons outlined here would be best taught as a cross-curricular project linking literacy and D&T as the children design and make their light. Practical tasks could be carried out in D&T lessons and writing tasks in the literacy sessions.

Switching on

Learning objective

■ To evaluate advertisements for their purpose and audience.

Resources

■ Sheet A (page 96)

■ A collection of advertisements from magazines and newspapers

■ Sticky notes

What to do

Begin by asking the children what an advertisement is. Let them have a few minutes sharing their ideas with their neighbours before you take any suggestions. Move on to ask what they know about advertisements and how they differ from other forms of text. Map out what they already know on a large piece of paper to display in the classroom. (You may find out, for example, that they know very little about the linguistic devices used.)

Display an enlarged version of Sheet A. Ask them to tell you what they notice about the advertisement. What is it

for? How do they know? Who do they think it is aimed at – children, teenagers, mothers, grandparents? Where do they think they might see this advertisement – comics, magazines, newspapers, railway stations? (They need to relate this to the target audience.) As they give you their answers, annotate the text with their main points.

Continue the discussion by focusing the children's attention on the special features of a persuasive text by asking questions such as:

'What is the verb tense used?'

'What persuasive devices are used?' – rhetorical questions, adjectives, emotive words, alliteration and so on.

'How is the advertisement presented?' – pictures, different fonts, layout and so on.

Again, annotate the enlarged text with the children's points as they make them. Encourage the class to look out for these features and additional ones in other advertisements.

For the independent work, give pairs of children some advertisements from comics, magazines, newspapers and so on. Ask them to answer the following questions which you have previously written on the board:

What product is being advertised?

Who is it aimed at?

Where might you find this advert?

Is it a good advertisement? Why?/Why not?

What features of persuasive texts does it include?

The answers to these questions could be written by the children on sticky notes and stuck on to their advertisements.

Take the opportunity to work with a couple of groups. Look at an advertisement together, answering the questions and discussing the features of advertisements. Then let the children look at an advertisement in their pairs as you move onto the next group.

Plenary

Ask for several volunteer pairs to show the rest of the class their advertisement, telling the others what was being advertised, who the intended audience was and where they think it could be found.

Then ask the class what additional features of advertisements they have discovered – catchphrases, exaggerated claims, tactics for grabbing attention and so on.

Finish the lesson by telling the children that over the next few lessons they will look at a variety of advertisements to learn more about them and then design their own advertisement for the light they have been making in the design and technology lessons.

Revving up

Learning objectives

■ To analyse and categorise linguistic features used in advertisements.

■ To invent different catchphrases to advertise a product.

Resources

■ A video of television advertisements or a recording of radio advertisements

■ Strips of paper or cards, sticky-tack

■ A child's finished model light from design and technology

What to do

Before this lesson, the children will need to have completed the making of their new type of light as part of their design and technology lessons (Unit 4e).

Listen to or watch some advertisements from radio or television. What catchphrases were used? Write each one on a separate strip of paper or card. Ask the children to tell you any other catchphrases from advertisements they know. Add these to the cards. Some well known ones include:

'You can do it when you B&Q it!'

'Have a break; have a Kit-Kat.'

'Frosties. They're grrreat!'

Ask the children what it is that makes these catchphrases so catchy and memorable. Why do they remember them so easily? Write all their ideas on a chart as headings, (leaving plenty of space between them). You are aiming to make a list of linguistic features so you may need to add some of your own to make sure they are covered – such as rhyme, alliteration, puns, rhetorical questions and emotive language.

Hold up each of the catchphrase cards, one at a time, and ask the children to try and categorise it under the correct heading for the linguistic device used. Stick the catchphrase under the correct heading. For example, 'You can do it when you B&Q it!' is a rhyme. 'Why go anywhere else?' is a rhetorical question.

Look at the examples of advertisements the children have brought in from home. Give them a few minutes to discuss with their neighbour which heading they think their advertisement should be categorised under and then work round the class sticking their advertisements under the right linguistic heading. Bring the children's attention to the style of the lettering used, the colours, the fonts and the size. Discuss which advertisements use catchphrases that make exaggerated claims. Ask for the children's ideas on why manufacturers make these claims.

Next, display one of the children's finished model lights on a table. Tell them that they are all advertising executives and the lighting company has asked them to come up with a catchphrase for advertising this new product.

Show them how to transform one or two of the easier catchphrases into their own phrases for advertising the light. For example:

'Lights. They're brright!'

'You can brighten it, when you lighten it!'

'Who makes it bright…'

Then, move them on to thinking up their own.

'Make it bright; turn on the light.'

'Flick that switch!'

For their independent work, ask the children to draw the light they designed in the middle of a piece of paper and then to write a couple of catchphrases around their product. Although there are working individually, it is a good idea to let the children talk about their ideas and help each other with rhyming words and so on.

Once they have come up with two or three ideas, they can then test different ways of writing their catchphrase, using different colours, size of letters and letter shapes. If possible, one group of children could complete their work on a computer, experimenting with different fonts, sizes and colours.

Plenary

Share good pieces of work with the class and ask them what is good about them. The children will have the opportunity to incorporate these good ideas into their own design. Look for pictures of the product that are clear and simple, illustrating what the purpose of the product is. Share catchphrases that rhyme, play on words, make an exaggerated claim or are examples of alliteration. Show catchphrases that are easy to read using large, bold letters in a clear colour.

Taking off

Learning objectives

■ To identify the different punctuation used in advertisements.

■ To write the text for an advertisement.

Resources

■ Sheet A (page 96)

■ A collection of advertisements from magazines and newspapers that have a variety of punctuation marks in the text (questions marks, exclamation marks, commas, semicolons, colons, dashes, hyphens and speech marks)

What to do

Look again at an enlarged version of Sheet A. Read it to the children and then explain that you want them to look at all the different types of punctuation used in the text. How many different ones can they find? List their names on the board and discuss the purpose of each one. Why do they think exclamation marks are used so much? Why do they think the sentences are so short? How does the punctuation help the reader?

Hand out the carefully selected collection of advertisements which have examples of the punctuation marks in the text – one advertisement between two or three children. Ask them to read it and then find an example of a punctuation mark you have been discussing.

Tell the children that for their independent work they will write their own text to advertise their invented light. Before they do this, discuss ideas about the following:

How long should the text be?

What claims is the text going to make?

What information does the text need to say?

What catchphrases will be used?

How will you use punctuation to good effect?

As you discuss each question, refer to the advertisement on Sheet A again and annotate it as a guide. Then, send the children off to draft their text. Make sure that all the children know that this means they are making a first copy of their text to write up at a later date, so handwriting and presentation are not as important as their ideas. Work with different groups highlighting good ideas and giving support where required.

Plenary

Share the children's ideas, commenting on good use of linguistic features, such as alliteration and rhyme as well as effective use of punctuation.

Finish the lesson by asking the children to work in pairs to look again at their text and check the punctuation in it. Do they need to add or delete any punctuation marks?

Flying solo

Learning objective

■ To design an advertisement.

Resources

■ A collection of advertisements from magazines and newspapers

What to do

Tell the children that today they are going to design and write their advertisement. Briefly remind them of the work they have completed in the previous lessons on:

■ use of pictures;

■ catchphrases, attention grabbing devices;

■ text and punctuation.

Tell them that now they need to put it all together and design their advertisement. Briefly look again at the collection of advertisements from magazines and newspapers to remind them about ideas and effects they can use in their own advertisements.

The advertisements could be designed using a suitable computer program.

Keep the introductory part of this lesson brief so that the children have plenty of time to share and complete their work.

Use the independent work time to circulate around the class, helping individual children and highlighting good work.

Plenary

End by displaying the children's finished advertisements and giving the class time to look closely at all of them.

Discuss with the children:

'Which catchphrases do you like? Why do you think they are effective?'

'Do any of the adverts use an exaggerated claim? Which advert do you like best? Why?'